NUTRITION AND HEALTH

VACCINES
THE TRUTH BEHIND THE DEBATES

BY MICHELLE HARRIS

Portions of this book originally appeared in
Vaccines by Kevin Hillstrom.

LUCENT PRESS

Published in 2020 by
Lucent Press, an Imprint of Greenhaven Publishing, LLC
353 3rd Avenue
Suite 255
New York, NY 10010

Designer: Deanna Paternostro
Editor: Jennifer Lombardo

Cataloging-in-Publication Data

Names: Harris, Michelle.
Title: Vaccines: The Truth Behind the Debates / Michelle Harris.
Description: New York : Lucent Press, 2020. | Series: Nutrition and Health | Includes glossary and index.
Identifiers: ISBN 9781534568839 (pbk.) | ISBN 9781534568747 (library bound) | ISBN 9781534568785 (ebook)
Subjects: LCSH: Vaccines–Juvenile literature. | Vaccination–Juvenile literature. | Vaccination–Social aspects–Juvenile literature.
Classification: LCC RA638.H332 2020 | DDC 615.3'72–dc23

Printed in China

Some of the images in this book illustrate individuals who are models. The depictions do not imply actual situations or events.

CPSIA compliance information: Batch #BW20KL: For further information contact Greenhaven Publishing LLC, New York, New York at 1-844-317-7404.

Please visit our website, www.greenhavenpublishing.com. For a free color catalog of all our high-quality books, call toll free 1-844-317-7404 or fax 1-844-317-7405.

CONTENTS

FOREWORD

People often want to do whatever they can to live healthy lives, but this is frequently easier said than done. For example, experts suggest minimizing stress as it takes a long-term toll on the body and mind. However, in an era where young adults must balance school attendance, extracurricular and social activities, and several hours of homework each night, stress is virtually unavoidable. Socioeconomic factors also come into play, which can prevent someone from making good health choices even when they are aware of what the consequences will be.

Other times, however, the problem is misinformation. The media frequently reports watered-down versions of scientific findings, distorting the message and causing confusion. Sometimes multiple conflicting results are reported, leaving people to wonder whether a simple action such as eating dark chocolate is helpful, harmful, or has no effect on their health at all. In such an environment, many people ignore all health news and decide for themselves what the best course of action is. This has led to dangerous trends such as the recent anti-vaccination movement.

The titles in the Nutrition and Health series aim to give young adults the information they need to take charge of their health. Factual, unbiased text presents all sides of current health issues with the understanding that everyone is different and knows their own body and health needs best. Readers also gain insight into important nutrition topics, such as whether a vegetarian diet is right for them, which foods may improve or exacerbate any existing health issues, and precautions they can take to prevent the spread of foodborne illnesses.

Annotated quotes from medical experts provide accurate and accessible explanations of challenging concepts, as well as different points of view on controversial issues. Additional books and websites are listed, giving readers a starting point from which to delve deeper into specific topics that are of interest to them. Full-color photographs, fact boxes, and enlightening charts are presented alongside the informative text to give young adults a clearer picture of today's most pressing health concerns.

With so much complicated and conflicting information about nutrition and health available on social media and in the news, it can be hard for all people—but especially for young adults—to make smart choices about their health. However, this series presents an accessible approach to health education that makes the work of staying healthy seem much less intimidating.

THE BEST DEFENSE IS A STRONG OFFENSE

Infectious diseases have been one of the greatest threats to human life throughout history—from the deadly smallpox virus, which arrived in the Americas in 1520 and killed millions, to the 1918 flu pandemic, which killed at least 50 million people worldwide. However, the frequency and impact of such infectious disease outbreaks has dropped dramatically in the past few decades. This is due in part to the development and distribution of immunity-boosting substances called vaccines. Typically delivered via injection, vaccines help prevent the spread of disease by rousing a person's immune system into action without actually making them sick. Vaccination has helped reduce the number of cases of dreaded diseases such as rubella, diphtheria, and whooping cough, as well as the paralyzing disease polio, which has been declared eradicated in the United States and in several other developed countries. The once-feared smallpox was defeated by vaccination; it was declared completely eradicated by the World Health Organization (WHO) in 1980 following a global vaccination campaign.

Vaccination has been so effective, in fact, that entire generations of Americans have grown up without any firsthand knowledge of the terror and heartache that some of these diseases caused. Most kids and parents in the United States now treat getting their shots as a routine part of growing up, similar to going to the dentist or getting a driver's license. According to the Program for Appropriate Technology in Health (PATH), a nonprofit organization that works to make vaccination available to low-income people around the world, "Only 50 years after vaccination became a standard rite of passage for children, it was taken for granted that a child born in the developed world would grow up without fear from the paralysis, brain damage, blindness and death that plagued the generations before her."[1]

In recent years, though, the wisdom of vaccination has been openly questioned, especially in the United States. Some parents and pediatricians argue that U.S. immunization programs, which now provide vaccines for 16 different diseases, have become too hard on kids. People who hold this view believe the vaccinations are given too close together and should be spread out more. Other critics say that government requirements regarding vaccination are an attack on their personal freedoms. Meanwhile, growing numbers of parents and politicians have claimed that vaccination

Some politicians, such as Kentucky senator Rand Paul, consider vaccination to be a parent's personal choice. In 2015, he made unproven claims that children have developed mental disorders after receiving some vaccines to back up his position that there should be no laws requiring children to get vaccinated.

is a key factor in the rise in autism, attention-deficit/hyperactivity disorder (ADHD), and other childhood developmental disorders.

Many scientists, doctors, and policymakers have reacted to these complaints with a mixture of anger and frustration. They continue to defend vaccines as one of the greatest and most beneficial tools of modern medicine. In their view, attacks on immunization programs are based on fear and ignorance, not accurate science. They also worry that as growing numbers of Americans choose not to vaccinate their children, the vulnerability to dangerous outbreaks of disease will grow. Their assurances, though, have failed to comfort critics. In fact, the debate over vaccination seems to grow more heated with each passing year.

Chapter One
HOW VACCINATION CHANGED HISTORY

The pages of history books are riddled with stories of devastating disease outbreaks, such as bubonic plague in the year 541—an outbreak that killed approximately 25 million people in the Roman Empire. This type of relatively localized outbreak is called an epidemic. Before the development of vaccines, people could do little to prevent epidemics or their destructive consequences.

In some cases, infectious diseases such as typhoid fever, smallpox, typhus, and bubonic plague spread so far that they devastated one or more entire continents. These continent-wide or global events are known as pandemics. The worst pandemic in history as of 2019 was an outbreak of bubonic plague that swept across medieval Europe and Asia in the 14th century. Scholars believe that this outbreak, known as the Black Death, may have cut Europe's entire population in half by the time it ran its course.

The world's early civilizations were largely helpless in the face of these horrifying events. They understood that smallpox, bubonic plague, and other terrors could be passed from person to person, but they did not know exactly how; for example, one widespread theory was that it had to do with bad smells. They also recognized that people who caught a disease such as smallpox and managed to survive did not have to worry about getting it again. They had no concept of germs or immune systems, however, and did not possess the scientific knowledge to protect themselves. When outbreaks of infectious disease occurred, their options were limited. All communities could do was separate the infected people from the uninfected ones—a practice known as quarantine—until they recovered. Some individuals and families, meanwhile, responded by fleeing to more lightly populated regions where they hoped the disease would not follow.

During the Black Death, doctors wore masks similar to this one because they believed it would protect them from infection. Because they thought the disease was spread through bad smells in the air, they put flowers and other sweet-smelling plants in the beak of the mask. Unfortunately, the masks did nothing to prevent the spread of the germs that were the real cause of the disease.

Many people, however, simply decided that they were at the mercy of God when disease entered their neighborhoods and homes. They comforted sick family members as best they could, then waited anxiously to see who would survive. As scholar Arthur Allen wrote, they lived in "a world in which loved ones were swept away by diseases whose sudden appearance was as mysterious as their departure."[2]

Early Inoculation Efforts

Feelings of powerlessness toward the world's scariest infectious diseases did not begin to change until the early 18th century. In 1721, a minister in Boston, Massachusetts, named Cotton Mather insisted that people actually had the ability to protect themselves from smallpox, which at that very moment was spreading terror and death across the city. Mather had heard about a practice called variolation that had been used for centuries in some parts of Africa and Asia to fight smallpox. Under this procedure, which later came to be known as inoculation, living smallpox virus was harvested directly from sick patients. This was done by taking scabs or liquid pus from the pustules, or skin sores, that typically erupted across the bodies of smallpox victims. The virus was then scratched into a healthy person's skin with a knife, needle, or other sharp instrument.

At first glance, the idea of deliberately infecting a healthy person with a deadly virus in order to protect them from that disease seemed ridiculous. Modern scientists know, though, that this process actually worked. These ancient African and Asian communities had figured out a way to expose healthy people to a weakened, less dangerous version of the disease-causing virus. Only a small amount of the virus was used in variolation, and it was introduced on an arm or leg, far away from the body's important organs such as the heart or lungs. In contrast, people who contracted smallpox from another person rather than through variolation typically suffered massive exposure through the respiratory system, which also gave the disease an easy avenue to attack vital organs and other body systems.

Once the immune system was awakened through variolation, it would then begin generating antibodies—the proteins that defend against dangerous germs when they enter people's bodies. Variolation could still make people sick for a few days or weeks, but the symptoms were not nearly as severe as they would be with a full-blown case of smallpox. Once the

A Presidential Pox

Three U.S. presidents are known to have contracted and survived smallpox infections, although only one was president when he got sick. George Washington caught the disease while visiting Barbados, a country in the Caribbean, in November 1751 when he was 19 years old. Andrew Jackson became infected with smallpox while being held prisoner by the British during the American Revolution, and though he survived, his brother did not. Finally, shortly after delivering his famous Gettysburg Address in 1863, President Abraham Lincoln became ill with smallpox and had to be quarantined. He recovered in about three weeks and went on to successfully lead the country through the American Civil War, which ended in 1865.

Abraham Lincoln was the only president to contract smallpox while he was in office.

patients recovered, they had lifelong immunity to the disease. This meant they could never experience the symptoms again; their immune system had learned how to defeat the smallpox germs and could kill them as soon as they entered the person's body.

Mather was so fascinated by the reports that he questioned slaves about whether they had ever undergone variolation back in Africa. After interviewing several slaves who had been inoculated successfully, Mather became convinced that the procedure could save Boston from the terror of smallpox once and for all. In the spring of 1721, he called for a city-wide variolation campaign against the disease. Many Boston residents were horrified by the suggestion, and most of the city's doctors criticized him.

Fortunately for Bostonians, Mather did manage to persuade one doctor to take part in the experiment. Zabdiel Boylston began variolating patients on June 26, 1721, starting with his 13-year-old son. He eventually completed the procedure on 248 patients.

The variolation campaign undertaken by Mather and Boylston sparked the creation of a large and vocal anti-variolation movement led by William Douglass, who was Boston's most respected doctor at the time. Douglass and his allies insisted that variolation would just make the epidemic worse. In fact, they described Mather's campaign as a potential threat to the city's very existence. Tensions over variolation eventually became so heated that Mather's enemies burned down his home.

As it turned out, Douglass's main accusation—that variolation did not work—was wrong. Scientists agree, though, that another one of Douglass's criticisms of the Mather-Boylston inoculation campaign was valid. Douglass regularly complained that neither Mather nor Boylston required patients who underwent variolation to be placed under quarantine. He correctly warned that this was unwise because freshly inoculated patients with smallpox in their systems had the potential to pass the disease along to people around them who had not been inoculated.

By the time the smallpox outbreak ran its course in early 1722, nearly 6,000 Boston residents had contracted the disease and more than 840 of them had died of it. Mather and Boylston, though, argued that the outbreak would have been even more severe had it not been for their variolation efforts. In 1726, they released a study indicating that 14 percent of Bostonians who had contracted smallpox naturally during the outbreak had died from the disease, while only 3 percent of Boylston's variolation patients had died. At first, Douglass and other critics dismissed these findings. As the 1720s unfolded, however, scientific and medical interest in variolation

A Closer Look

Although it is the same process as vaccination, variolation refers specifically to inoculation with smallpox, not with any other disease. This is because the term comes from the word variola—the scientific name for the virus that causes smallpox.

grew considerably. By 1730, when the next smallpox epidemic rolled into Boston, Douglass was among the city's most vocal supporters of variolation.

Drawbacks of Variolation

Variolation slowly became more popular throughout the 18th century as doctors around the world saw the impact it could have in reducing the virus's spread in their communities.

For centuries, doctors and other health care practitioners had only treated patients after they fell victim to a disease. With variolation, though, they could take action to protect patients before an epidemic even broke out. By the mid-1700s, this early landmark in preventive medicine was being practiced to one degree or another in Philadelphia, Boston, New York, and other big American cities prone to smallpox outbreaks. Acceptance was also on the rise in the biggest cities in Europe.

Despite this growing acceptance, variolation campaigns continued to be viewed with skepticism and suspicion, especially when some minor smallpox outbreaks were traced to variolated patients who had not been properly quarantined. Sometimes variolation did not work because the fluid drained from a smallpox pustule for use in variolation was too old to make variolation effective. Other times, it was contaminated with tetanus, syphilis, or other bacteria that could sicken or kill people who agreed to undergo variolation.

Numerous doctors also added many unnecessary—and sometimes dangerous—preparations to the variolation process. Even the best doctors of the era had only a limited understanding of disease and immunity. They often recommended medical treatments to be done before variolation that were deeply flawed—sometimes to the point of being dangerous to the patient. Other doctors were simply greedy, ordering pre-variolation procedures so they could charge more money.

Pre-variolation treatments took many forms. For example, patients who were being prepared for variolation were frequently given doses of mercury, a chemical that could cause diarrhea and brain damage. Others were given a chemical called calomel, which could loosen teeth to the point that they fell out. John Adams, the second president of the United States, endured both of these treatments when he was prepared for variolation in the winter of 1764. "[My doctors] reduced me very low before they performed the operation," Adams recalled in his autobiography. "Every tooth in my head became so loose that I believe I could have pulled them all with my Thumb and finger."[3]

Other popular pre-variolation treatments included weeks of bloodletting—a process in which doctors would purposely cut patients to reduce the amount of blood in their bodies. Doctors at the time believed this put the body in better "balance." Another treatment involved daily infusions of medicines that caused heavy vomiting. Many people were forced to endure all of these treatments at the same time. Scholars believe that these preparations weakened some patients so much that they were in danger of dying from even a weak dose of smallpox by the time the day of variolation finally came around.

The medical profession finally moved away from these damaging preparatory treatments in the late 1700s. This change helped improve the reputation of variolation, as did the public support of leading politicians such as Thomas Jefferson and Benjamin Franklin. Another big factor was General George Washington's decision to order that the entire Continental Army be variolated in 1777, at the height of the American Revolution. This campaign was so successful in reducing smallpox cases among Washington's troops that it has been credited as a factor in America's victory over the British Empire.

By the end of the 1700s, many—though not all—Americans had come around to the idea that variolation provided both protection and peace of mind. As a scholar from Philadelphia wrote, "Over the course of a century, inoculation had transformed smallpox from the dreaded scourge [curse] known as the 'speckled monster' to a guest encouraged to visit the family home."[4]

The World's First Vaccine

In 1796, physician Edward Jenner made an extraordinary discovery that seemingly had no explanation: Milkmaids almost never contracted smallpox. In trying to figure out why this might be, Jenner theorized that the farmworkers had all previously contracted cowpox from the cows they milked and that the two illnesses were similar enough that immunity to one—granted through fighting off the illness—was enough to create immunity for the other, more serious infection.

Jenner tested his hypothesis on a local eight-year-old boy named James Phipps by taking pus from a cowpox sore on a milkmaid's hand

Edward Jenner is credited with creating the first vaccine.

and placing it in a fresh cut on the boy's arm. Phipps became feverish and achy from this treatment, which later came to be called vaccination. The name came from *vaccinia*, the Latin term for cowpox. He recovered in a matter of days, though, and six weeks later Jenner variolated the boy with smallpox. When the boy remained perfectly healthy, Jenner knew that he had discovered a medical treatment that would change the world.

Jenner conducted a series of other successful vaccination experiments on local farming families using lymph—a bodily fluid—taken directly from infected cows. He then published his findings in a book called *An Inquiry into the Causes and Effects of the Variolae Vaccinae*. Jenner's explanation of the cowpox vaccine and its power to stop smallpox took the world by storm. Within a few years, the so-called Jennerian inoculation was spreading across Europe and America. Millions of people volunteered to be vaccinated with cowpox, and Jenner became an international celebrity. "Every friend of humanity must look with pleasure on this discovery, by which one evil more is withdrawn from the condition of man,"[5] wrote Thomas Jefferson.

Jenner's cowpox vaccine was a clear improvement on the old, risky technique of variolation because it did not rely on immunization through exposure to actual smallpox. However, vaccination had its own problems. One 1800 vaccination campaign in Massachusetts had tragic results when vaccinators accidentally used smallpox rather than cowpox, killing 68 people. Other vaccinations ended up providing no smallpox protection because the cowpox lymph was too old. A number of vaccines spread different diseases because they had been contaminated with syphilis or other blood-borne illnesses.

Finally, some parents, doctors, and ministers objected to the vaccine on religious grounds. Jenner's reliance on lymph from an animal led them to make the accusation that vaccination was not natural and therefore not what God wanted them to do. Some opponents falsely claimed that vaccinated children showed signs of sprouting cows' horns. An organization known as the Anti-Vaccination Society called vaccination "a gross violation of religion, law, morality, and humanity."[6] In an illustration in one 1806 book, Jenner was drawn "with a tail and hoofs, feeding basketsful of infants to a hideous monster."[7]

When Mandatory Vaccination Became Law

With the success of the smallpox vaccine, many governments felt it was in the best interest of their nations to legally require all citizens to be vaccinated against the highly infectious and devastating disease. Great Britain passed a series of mandatory vaccination laws between 1840 and 1873 despite loud objections from some of its citizens. In 1874, Germany passed a law requiring all German children to receive smallpox vaccinations by age 2, with follow-up vaccinations around age 12.

Federal authorities in the United States were more reluctant to make mandatory vaccination laws, but a number of city and state lawmakers approved them. In addition, a growing number of America's public schools made vaccination a condition of student enrollment: If a student had not been vaccinated, they were not welcome in the classroom. This rule was instituted in several big cities that were particularly vulnerable to epidemics.

A Closer Look

Following an extensive vaccination initiative in 1972, smallpox was eliminated from the United States. In fact, according to the website Healthline, vaccinations for that particular disease are no longer necessary in the country.

The mandatory, or compulsory, vaccination movement was supported by several historical developments. In both the American Civil War in the 1860s and Europe's Franco-Prussian War in the late 1880s, the eventual victors benefited greatly from their superior smallpox vaccination programs. Around this same time, the supply of high-quality smallpox vaccine soared with the creation of so-called vaccine farms. At these farms, which became popular in both the United States and Europe, large numbers of cattle were kept specifically to provide a steady flow of cowpox lymph that could be used in vaccines.

Another major improvement in vaccine quality was made in the 1880s by German scientist Robert Koch and his talented staff of researchers. They discovered that when cowpox lymph was stored in a chemical called glycerin, other dangerous germs that were sometimes present in the vaccine, such as tetanus, syphilis, and *Streptococci*, were killed off. In addition, thinning the virus in glycerin made it possible for doctors to make the vaccine last longer, so more people could be inoculated with a single batch. According to Allen, "A single cow could now yield up to 6,000 vaccinations, compared with 200 to 300 doses per cow with unglycerinated vaccine."[8]

Public acceptance of vaccination also received a big boost from the famous French scientist Louis Pasteur. In the early 1880s, Pasteur developed a vaccine that was effective in combating chicken cholera, which had long been a serious problem for French poultry farmers. A few years later, in 1885, Pasteur unveiled a vaccine for rabies, a relatively rare but much-feared disease that people contract from the saliva of infected animals, generally by being bitten. Meanwhile, Pasteur's decision to follow Jenner's example and call his medicines "vaccines" catapulted the word into common usage. From this point forward, "vaccine" became the term used for any medicine designed to trigger immunity to a specific disease.

Further research led to the development of other vaccines. In 1888, French biologist Émile Roux discovered the diphtheria toxin, paving the way for the development of a diphtheria antitoxin by the end of the century. Antitoxins are medicines similar to vaccines that prevent someone from getting a disease after they have been exposed to certain poisonous microorganisms, or germs, rather than before they encounter them. Around the same time, French scientist Alexandre Yersin identified the specific form of bacterium responsible for bubonic plague. In 1893, Russian bacteriologist Waldemar Mordecai Haffkine unveiled the first cholera vaccine. Although it needed work, it helped make a cholera epidemic in India slightly less deadly. Later versions of the vaccine were more effective.

Vaccination Goes to Court

Both the United States and Great Britain experienced resistance to mandatory vaccination. However, in the early 20th century, the two countries began to take very different approaches to combat this resistance.

In England, opposition to compulsory vaccination among the poor and working class became so strong that the country's political leadership backed off. In 1898, Parliament passed a law that permitted people to reject vaccination if they said they did not believe in it. Newspapers and vaccination opponents, meanwhile, circulated every horror story they could find about vaccinations that caused death. Such scare tactics resulted in a severe reduction in vaccination rates. By 1914, only half of England's population had been vaccinated for smallpox—a far cry from the 80 percent vaccination rate of 1898.

In the United States, smallpox vaccination became mandatory in a growing number of public schools. Many cities and states also adopted

COMPULSORY VACCINATION ACT.
(16 & 17 Victoria, Cap. 100.)

SCHEDULE A.

Medical Certificate of Successful Vaccination.
[To be delivered (pursuant to Section IV.) to the Father or Mother of every Child successfully Vaccinated, or to the Person having the Care, Nurture, or Custody of such Child.]

I, the undersigned, hereby certify, That (a)________ (aged (b) 7 [illegible]), the Child of (c)________ of (d) [and residing at No.____ in ________ Street in] the Parish of ________ in the County of ________ has been successfully vaccinated by me.

Dated this (e) ____ day of ____ 1860.

(*Signature of the Person certifying*)________

(*Add Professional Titles*)________

[☞ See Note on the other side.]

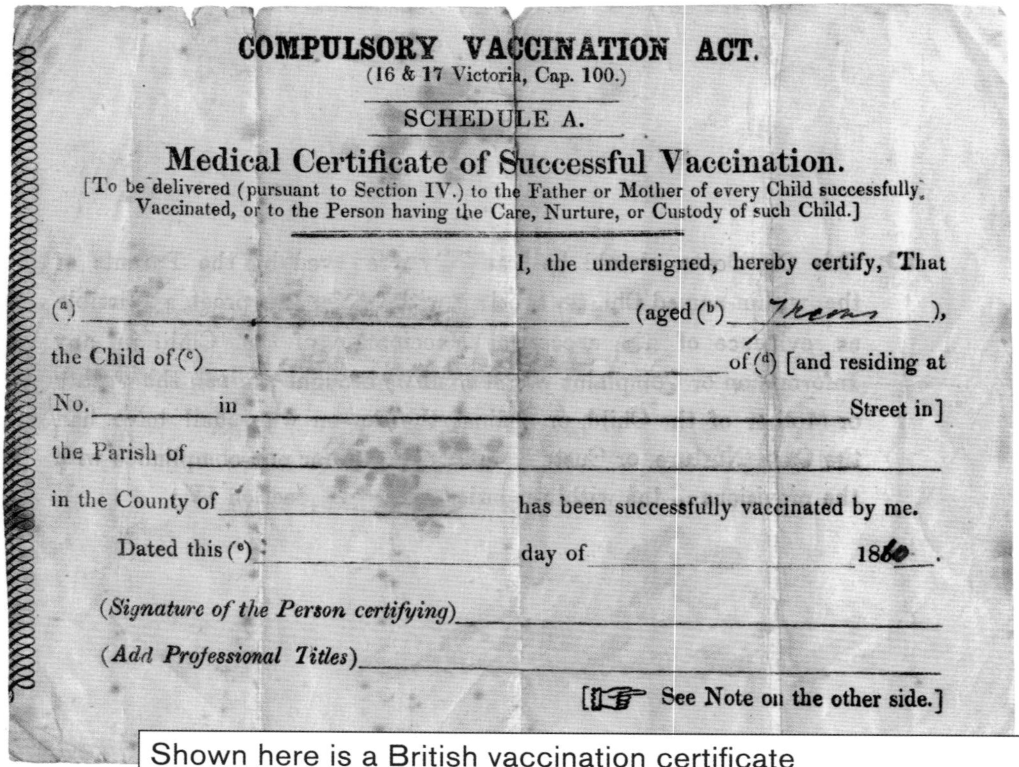

Shown here is a British vaccination certificate from the 1800s. Doctors signed them and gave them to the parents so they could prove their children had been vaccinated.

compulsory vaccination laws. Public attitudes toward this trend remained mixed, though, in large part because of persistent fears about the safety of vaccines. These concerns intensified when parents heard reports such as the ones that came out of Philadelphia and nearby Camden, New Jersey, in late 1901, when 90 residents of these cities—most of them children—died after doctors vaccinated them for smallpox, unaware that the vaccine had been contaminated with the deadly bacterium *Clostridium tetani*, which causes tetanus.

Public shock about the 1901 tetanus disaster finally convinced the U.S. Congress to take steps to make sure that American vaccines were being made, shipped, and stored properly. Up to this point, reported John F. Anderson of the U.S. Public Health Service, "anyone could make a product, label it vaccine virus and place it on the market."[9] With the passage of the

1902 Biologics Control Act, federal agencies were authorized to oversee the production of vaccines. Manufacturers had to earn licenses from the U.S. Public Health Service (PHS) to sell vaccines and antitoxins. Within a few years of the 1902 legislation, one-third of all U.S. vaccine makers had been forced to shut their doors because they could not meet the new PHS safety standards. The remaining companies were held to higher quality standards than ever before.

The move toward compulsory vaccination was also aided by the U.S. Supreme Court. In a 1905 case called *Jacobson v. Massachusetts*, the Court ruled that states had the right to insist on immunization—the process of making a person immune to a disease, often through the use of vaccines—because the need to protect community public health outweighed individual Americans' right to privacy.

The Devastating Toll of Contagious Diseases

The early 20th century brought several reminders of the devastating effects of infectious disease. Paralytic polio killed thousands and paralyzed even more, while typhus tore through the battlefields of Europe during World War I. Before the dust had settled from the war, a virulent form of influenza, or flu, spread worldwide. The 1918 Spanish flu was the worst influenza pandemic in recent recorded history, infecting approximately 500 million people and killing at least 50 million—675,000 in the United States alone. According to the Centers for Disease Control and Prevention (CDC), more people died during the 1918 pandemic than the total number of military and civilian deaths that resulted from World War I.

Despite such setbacks, though, the United States made continued progress in its efforts to eradicate, or completely get rid of, infectious diseases. In 1914, a rabies vaccine was licensed for use in the United States, and one year later, vaccines for both typhoid fever and pertussis—also called whooping cough—became available on the U.S. market. The U.S. military also ordered mandatory typhoid vaccinations for all American troops. This precaution proved to be a wise one; the United States suffered far fewer losses from typhoid during World War I than the other armies did. Typhoid fever took only 227 American lives during the war; in contrast, the French military lost 12,000 soldiers to the disease in the first 16 months of the conflict. This horrible death toll convinced French authorities to order their own mandatory vaccination program.

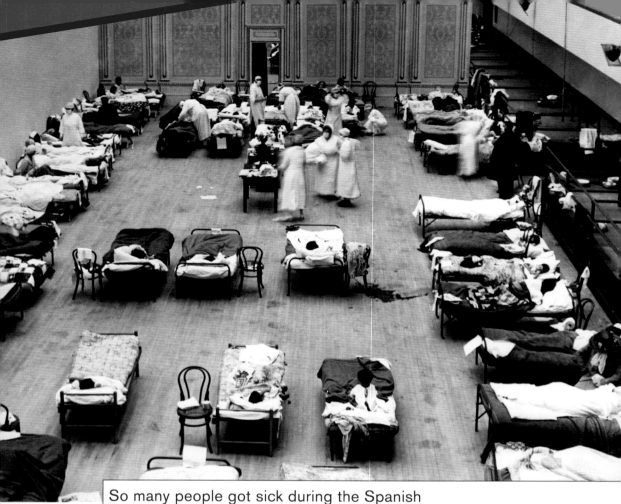

So many people got sick during the Spanish flu pandemic that makeshift hospitals such as this one had to be set up to hold them all.

Vaccination's reputation benefited as well from steadily growing faith in American medicine and science. "During the 1920s and 1930s scientists and physicians continued to make breathtaking gains in their ability to recognize and combat disease and other forms of sickness," explained Kevin Hillstrom, author of the book *U.S. Health Politics and Policy*. "These advances in medical science … brought about significant declines in outbreaks of infectious disease; increased reliance on both simple and complex surgical procedures; and unprecedented levels of public confidence in the drugs, therapies, and procedures that physicians prescribed for patients."[10]

In other words, American parents gradually became more accepting of vaccination for the simple reason that it seemed to be working. Small-pox epidemics were fading in both intensity and frequency. From 1921 to 1930, for example, only 400,000 cases of smallpox were documented in the United States, and fewer than 1 percent of patients died. The numbers fell even more in the following decade.

Vaccination campaigns had a lot to do with those numbers. Scientists have since acknowledged, however, that these impressive results were aided by the fact that a milder strain of smallpox known as *V. minor* emerged in the early 20th century. Researchers believe that this type of smallpox, which became the most common strain in the United States through the 1940s, may have immunized many Americans against the more deadly version known as *V. major*.

A Closer Look

A strain of a bacterium or virus is a type that has genetic differences from other types of the same microorganism. It can be compared to ice cream flavors: Chocolate ice cream with mint and chocolate ice cream with peanut butter are two different "strains" of chocolate ice cream.

Building a Healthier America

In the beginning of the 20th century, the United States began to make great strides in improving the health and safety of its citizens. In addition to medical innovations—including new and improved vaccines, technologies, and surgical treatments—the government passed new laws and regulations to increase the safety of the country's food and water supplies. Thanks to these efforts, the life expectancy for the average American increased by nearly 25 percent in just 30 years.

During the post-World War I years, the anti-vaccination movement faded in influence across most of the United States. Most parents raising families in cities and large towns seemed to accept that immunizing their children was a low-risk and sensible precaution. In New York City, for example, a diphtheria immunization effort vaccinated half a million children from 1929 to 1931 with little protest. Opponents of compulsory vaccination did not find a sympathetic ear in Washington, D.C., either. When one critic appeared before Congress to complain about the practice, Michigan congressman Roy O. Woodruff responded by citing statistics indicating that typhoid, diphtheria, and other infectious diseases were not nearly the threat they once were. "How anybody having these figures before him can be opposed to vaccination and the prevention of disease is more than I can understand," Woodruff said to the vaccination critic. "If your ideas prevailed in this country, we would still have smallpox, typhoid, and other epidemics which have now almost entirely disappeared."[11]

By the 1930s, though, public health officials warned that the great strides that America had made in combating infectious disease were giving some people too much confidence. As the rate of disease decreased, so did the vaccination rate; it seemed as though people had forgotten the reason why disease was no longer such a threat. During that decade, only nine states had compulsory vaccination laws in place, and in the absence of a legal requirement, many people were choosing not to get their children vaccinated.

Vaccination in the Armed Forces

This overconfidence ended as another great war broke out in Europe. As American troops prepared to ship out to join the Allied forces against Germany and Japan in World War II, the U.S. government started a special agency, known as the Armed Forces Epidemiological Board, to protect them against infectious disease. The organization invested large amounts of money and resources into vaccine research, focusing on infectious illnesses such as tetanus, yellow fever, and typhus.

Around the same time, scientists around the world developed insecticides such as DDT, which wiped out huge numbers of malaria-carrying mosquitoes and typhus-carrying lice. In fact, DDT applications were credited with virtually eradicating typhus in many parts of Europe; however, the chemical's deadly impact on bird populations and other aspects of the natural environment would not be discovered until 20 years later. Medical researchers also discovered how to mass-produce penicillin, a medicine discovered in 1928 that proved amazingly effective at fighting bacterial infections.

Vaccinating members of the military has always been a priority for the United States.

By the time the war ended in 1945, appreciation for vaccines and other "miracle medicines" had reached new heights. "Vaccination had put a sanitary shield around our men, protecting them from the scourges of previous wars: typhoid fever, tetanus, smallpox, cholera, typhus, and plague," explained Allen. "Yes, the shots hurt and even caused illness sometimes, but the soldier survived. Returning from the war he wanted his children to have the same protection."[12] After the war, in fact, many Americans came to see getting vaccinated as an important patriotic duty.

Americans were also quick to line up for vaccinations when confronted with the threat of a genuine epidemic. When a case of smallpox was documented in New York City in April 1947, for example, 6 million residents voluntarily submitted to vaccination in the space of three weeks. This prompt response ended the outbreak before it had a chance to spread. America's last known outbreak of smallpox occurred two years later in Texas and was quickly contained.

The Pursuit of Polio's Demise

Incredible advancements in vaccine science were made during the 1950s and 1960s as scientists, lawmakers, and public health officials worked together to develop and distribute new vaccines. In this "golden age" of vaccination, experts created vaccines for such diseases as measles, hepatitis B, and tuberculosis, as well as the DTP (also known as DTaP) vaccine that protects against diphtheria, tetanus, and pertussis all in one injection.

The greatest vaccination achievement of this era was the development of a vaccine against polio, a contagious virus that generally struck during childhood and caused muscle weakness, breathing problems, and paralysis (an inability to move the muscles). Polio had loomed as a terrifying threat to parents since ancient times, but outbreaks had steadily worsened in the first few decades of the 20th century, killing or crippling many people. Even having enough money to see the finest doctors and live in the cleanest conditions was not enough to prevent someone from contracting polio.

A Closer Look

President Franklin Delano Roosevelt (FDR) is often cited as one of the most famous polio survivors. However, in 2003, a study published in the *Journal of Medical Biography* noted that FDR's symptoms were more consistent with the neurological condition Guillain-Barré syndrome (GBS). For example, while polio generally affects only one side of the body, FDR lost the use of both of his legs. GBS was a relatively unknown condition when FDR was diagnosed in 1921, while polio was a widespread epidemic, so the researchers believe FDR's doctors simply misdiagnosed him with a disease they were more familiar with. However, since no tests for polio were performed on FDR, no one will ever be able to say for sure what caused his paralysis.

By the 1940s, several teams of researchers around the globe were racing to see who could first develop a safe and effective vaccine against the disease, which came in three different strains. Parents in America, Europe, and around the world followed each twist and turn in this quest closely. "The largest medical experiment conducted in the world up to that time, it riveted the public attention like no other scientific event of the twentieth century,"[13] wrote James Colgrove in his book *State of Immunity: The Politics of Vaccination in Twentieth-Century America.*

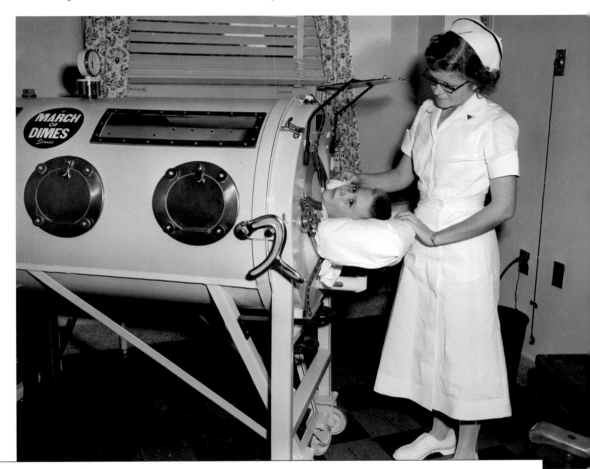

Shown here is a young polio patient in an iron lung. This machine helped people breathe normally when their chest muscles had been paralyzed.

Jonas Salk: A Medical Hero

Jonas Salk, a doctor and medical researcher, was an associate professor of bacteriology and director of the Virus Research Laboratory at the University

Janice Flood Nichols: Polio Survivor

Janice Flood Nichols, author of *Twin Voices: A Memoir of Polio, the Forgotten Killer*, was diagnosed with polio as a child. In the 1950s, many children caught polio; Nichols's twin brother and 8 out of their 24 classmates were diagnosed at the same time as Nichols. The disease killed her brother and three of her classmates, but Janice survived and became one of the pioneers who were given the first vaccine for the disease in 1954. She remembered,

> In spring 1954 (while still in the throes of intensive physical therapy), I was one of 1,829,916 children in the United States, Canada, and Finland who participated in the Salk vaccine trial, the largest vaccine trial in the history of the world. They called us "Polio Pioneers" as the successful production of a polio vaccine would benefit all present and future children—we were proud little kids! The following spring the vaccine was licensed. So vital was this vaccine that President Dwight Eisenhower signed an executive order to provide manufacturing protocol to 75 nations free of charge. Today the world is close to global polio eradication, but the disease remains endemic [commonly diagnosed] in three countries. A few years ago, nearly half of the world's cases took place in the European Region. For this reason, public health professionals remind us that polio is a disease that is just a plane trip away, ready to pounce on un-vaccinated children and adults.[1]

1. Janice Flood Nichols, "Unprotected People #105: Polio," Immunization Action Coalition, accessed on April 24, 2019. www.immunize.org/reports/report105.pdf.

of Pittsburgh School of Medicine when he began to develop the techniques that would lead to a vaccine for polio. Previously, Salk had been part of the team that developed a vaccine for two serious types of influenza during World War II. In 1952, he began field tests of his vaccine, which was made up of "killed" polio. It proved successful in raising antibody levels without giving any subjects the disease itself. National testing of the vaccine began two years later when one million children, who were known as the "Polio Pioneers," were immunized.

On April 12, 1955, authorities announced that Salk's vaccine was 80 to 90 percent effective against paralytic polio. The U.S. government immediately approved the vaccine for public use, and immunization began within a matter of weeks. Unfortunately, the immunization program was halted

Shown here is Jonas Salk. His polio vaccine resulted in the complete eradication of the disease from the United States, saving millions of people from paralysis or death.

after it was discovered that one of the six polio vaccine makers, Cutter Laboratories, had produced a vaccine that used live poliovirus instead of a dead form of the disease. This tragedy, which became known as the Cutter incident, resulted in the deaths of 10 people and the permanent paralysis of 200 others. It also sickened thousands of other inoculated children.

Once investigators figured out that the Cutter incident stemmed from the lab's carelessness and too little government supervision—not from any problem with Salk's vaccine—the national immunization campaign resumed. By the end of 1957, more than 200 million doses of the vaccine had been administered through massive immunization programs. Cases of polio fell dramatically all around the world. In the United States, for instance, the annual number of polio cases fell from more than 38,000 in 1954 to 910 by 1962. By the early 2000s, polio had been completely eradicated across the United States.

In the late 1950s, American researcher Albert Sabin created a "live-virus" polio vaccine that eventually became more popular than Salk's creation. Sabin's version was easier to give to patients: It could be eaten with a sugar cube, while Salk's vaccine required a shot. It also produced a quicker immune response, which meant that it was more effective in the case of a sudden outbreak of the virus.

Nonetheless, Salk is still given credit today as the scientist who first came up with an effective immunization against polio. "I was nine when the polio vaccine came out," recalled one American doctor. "Dr. Salk was in the news and my parents talked about him. They were so glad, so relieved, we could get this vaccine … Salk was a hero. I remember thinking this was something wonderful, to be a doctor and help people. I went into medicine because of Dr. Salk."[14]

Potential Harm from Vaccination

Vaccination programs eventually expanded worldwide thanks to international organizations such as WHO and the United Nations Children's Fund (UNICEF), as well as major philanthropic organizations such as the Rockefeller Foundation, Rotary International, and the Bill and Melinda Gates Foundation. These campaigns have helped turn many devastating diseases, including polio and smallpox, into mere memories in much of the world. Smallpox has been completely eradicated around the world, and in 1994, the WHO Region of the Americas was certified polio-free, followed by the

WHO Western Pacific Region in 2000 and the WHO European Region in June 2002. Whooping cough, measles, mumps, diphtheria, and other diseases that people previously lived in fear of contracting were "reduced from frightening epidemics to rare outbreaks within a few decades."[15]

Beginning in the 1970s, though, vaccination also came under renewed attack in the United States. These criticisms increased in intensity and volume throughout the remainder of the 1900s and have remained strong in the 21st century. Some critics have claimed that certain vaccines have outlived their usefulness or that they pose unnecessary health risks to children. Anti-vaccination groups have claimed, for example, that vaccines might be responsible for rising rates of autism, a disorder that hinders the development of social and communication skills in children.

Vaccination begins soon after a child is born. This has caused some parents to make false connections between the vaccine and changes in their baby's phyiscal and mental health.

Debunking the Autism Link

A 1998 study published in the British medical journal the *Lancet* alleged that the chemical thimerosal, which was used in the standard vaccine for measles, mumps, and rubella (known as the MMR vaccine), might be contributing to increasing rates of autism in children. Immediately afterward, the scientific community launched additional studies to try to replicate these findings, but they were unable to do so. In fact, the *Lancet* issued a short retraction following the study's publication, stating that there had not been enough data to establish a clear link between the MMR vaccine and autism.

Numerous studies since then have found no link at all between the MMR vaccine and autism, though the fear persists due to the spread of false information on the internet and by celebrities—especially model, actress, and anti-vaccine activist Jenny McCarthy.

A study conducted in Denmark and published in March 2019 in *Annals of Internal Medicine* aimed to dispel this continuing myth in the hope of providing parents more assurance in the safety of the vaccine. The study—one of the largest studies ever done on the MMR vaccine—analyzed data collected from all children born in Denmark to Danish-born mothers between 1999 and 2010. From this analysis, researchers found that there was no overall increased risk for autism among those who received the MMR vaccine when compared with those who had not gotten the vaccine. The lead researcher, Anders Hviid, told National Public Radio (NPR),

> *The idea that vaccines cause autism is still around despite our original and other well-conducted studies ... We felt that it was time to revisit the link in a larger cohort with more follow-up which also allowed for more comprehensive analyses of different claims such as the idea that MMR causes autism in susceptible children ... Parents should not avoid vaccinating their children for fear of autism.*[1]

1. Quoted in Rob Stein, "A Large Study Provides More Evidence That MMR Vaccines Don't Cause Autism," NPR, March 4, 2019. www.npr.org/sections/health-shots/2019/03/04/699997613/a-large-study-provides-more-evidence-that-mmr-vaccines-dont-cause-autism.

Although vaccines are incredibly effective at preventing deadly diseases, they are not entirely without risk. Even the CDC states that, like any medication, vaccines can cause side effects. Most vaccine-related side effects are mild, such as pain or redness at the injection site, but more serious effects can sometimes occur. According to the CDC, "Serious side effects after vaccination, such as severe allergic reaction, are very rare and doctors and clinic staff are trained to deal with them."[16] However, severe side effects can be terrifying to parents of a recently immunized child regardless of how rarely they occur.

One mother named Amanda Mickelson said she felt guilty after her 10-month-old daughter, Riley, suffered brain damage following a DTaP vaccination. "There was no warning or indication of the danger. Twelve hours post vaccine injection, my daughter looked into my face as the life silently faded from her in an instant. The brain damage left her unresponsive and no longer breathing on her own. She turned an unmistakable shade of gray that will never be forgotten,"[17] wrote Amanda. After rushing her daughter to the hospital, a neurologist explained that the reaction was due to vaccine injury.

Vaccines are thoroughly tested for safety through scientific studies, which allow scientists to identify the most common side effects of a particular vaccine before it is licensed by the Food and Drug Administration (FDA), which oversees the purity and effectiveness of medications in the United States. However, these studies may not identify rare negative effects that can arise once millions of individuals begin to receive the vaccine. For this reason, the U.S. vaccine safety system continuously watches out for possible vaccine-related side effects, including those reported to the Vaccine Adverse Event Reporting System (VAERS). This is a national system used by scientists at the FDA and CDC to collect reports of possible side effects that happen after vaccination. Additionally, the 1986 National Childhood Vaccine Injury Act established the National Vaccine Injury Compensation Program (VICP), a federal no-fault system that offers monetary compensation to individuals or their families who experience injury or death by certain childhood vaccines. Between 1988 and 2017, the program paid out approximately $3.8 billion in compensation, according to the U.S. Department of Health and Human Services (HHS).

Growing numbers of American families have responded to these concerns by refusing to immunize their children. Prominent organizations such as the American Medical Association (AMA) and the American Academy of Pediatrics (AAP) have worked hard to reassure the public of the importance of full vaccination. According to WHO, serious injury from vaccination is extremely rare, occuring only once in every thousand or million vaccinations, and vaccine deaths are so rare that the risk cannot be accurately calculated because there is too little information. Thus far, however, these educational campaigns have had only a limited impact since the stories about these rare events tend to be sensationalized in the news. In contrast, news outlets do not report on the millions of people who receive vaccines and report no negative effects.

Chapter Two

AN INTRODUCTION TO VACCINES

Vaccines help protect people from deadly diseases by working with the body's natural defenses—the immune system—to increase immunity and decrease the risk of infection. Typically, when a bacterium or virus infects the body, the immune system automatically responds by calling in the troops (white blood cells) to fight the invading organisms with special proteins called antibodies. Once the infection is defeated, the body is unlikely to get sick from that same illness again because the antibodies remain in the bloodstream, always alert and ready to battle the invaders again. "Constant vigilance" is the immune system's motto. In order to prevent illness, therefore, vaccines work by tricking the immune system into thinking it is under attack by a particular disease, causing the white blood cells to rush into action and start creating antibodies that are designed specifically for that disease. "If these germs reappear, whether it's a few weeks or many years later, the antibodies are ready to protect," explained the website Healthy Children. "That's why if you had the mumps or measles as a child, you never got it again, no matter how often you were exposed to the same infectious agent."[18]

Because vaccines contain dead or severely weakened pathogens—another naeme for germs—they do not cause the same symptoms someone would experience if they had caught the actual disease. "In other words," the CDC explained, "a vaccine is a safer substitute for a child's first exposure to a disease ... Through vaccination, children can develop immunity without suffering from the actual diseases that vaccines prevent."[19] Effective vaccines also do not put any additional strain on the body's immune system since the immune system's entire job is to create antibodies for the various pathogens people encounter every day. The immune system is constantly fighting off disease without people even being aware of it.

Scientists do not use just one blueprint to create these vaccines, though. Over the years, they have developed vaccines using a wide range of methods and materials. Their approaches, according to the National Institute of Allergy and Infectious Diseases (NIAID), "are typically based on fundamental information about the microbe [germ], such as how it infects cells and how the immune system responds to it, as well as practical considerations, such as regions of the world where the vaccine would be used."[20] Whatever the circumstances, though, each vaccine has been carefully formulated to trigger the creation of antibodies that can provide immunized people with lasting protection against specific diseases. In many cases, this protection can last a lifetime. Other antibodies created by vaccines, though, fade in strength over time. This is why additional vaccinations, known as booster shots or booster doses, are recommended for some infectious diseases.

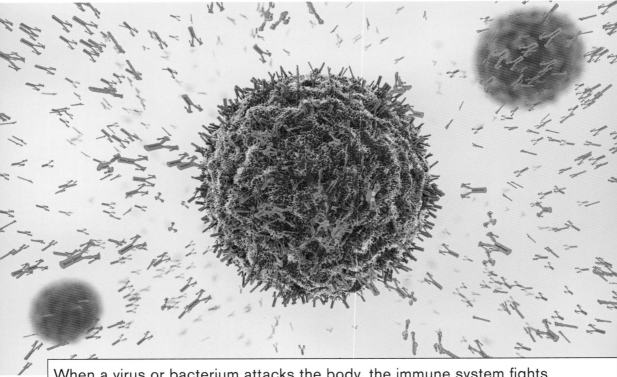

When a virus or bacterium attacks the body, the immune system fights it off by producing antibodies that are designed to attack that specific germ. Shown here is an illustration of antibodies attacking a virus.

It Takes a Herd

Herd immunity is a process by which everyone in a community is protected from infectious disease because enough members of the population are immune. The disease cannot spread or cause an outbreak because there are not enough other unvaccinated people to infect. Therefore, the more members of the "herd" who are vaccinated against infectious disease, the better the entire community is protected. Herd immunity is particularly important to protect the most vulnerable members of a community who are unable to be vaccinated, including children who are too young to be vaccinated yet; those whose immune systems do not work right, such as people who have acquired immunodeficiency syndrome (AIDS); and those who are too ill to be vaccinated, such as cancer patients.

In recent years, herd immunity against previously eradicated or contained diseases has been dangerously decreased by state laws allowing parents to choose not to vaccinate their children. Measles, for instance, had been declared eliminated in the United States in 2000, but low vaccination rates since then have led to various outbreaks of the potentially deadly disease all across the country.

In January 2019, health officials in Washington State declared a state of emergency due to an outbreak of measles that spread over two counties, infecting more than 30 individuals in a region with lower-than-normal vaccination rates. Two months later, officials in Rockland County, New York, banned unvaccinated children from public places, including schools and parks, for 30 days in an effort to combat a measles outbreak with 167 confirmed cases across the county. "We must not allow this outbreak to continue," said Rockland county executive Ed Day at a news conference, defending the ban. "We will not sit idly by while children in our community are at risk."[1] However, a judge stopped the ban after 10 days.

According to the CDC, more than 380 cases of measles were confirmed in 15 states within three months, between January 1 and March 28, 2019—the second-greatest number of cases reported in the United States since measles was declared eliminated in 2000.

1. Quoted in Frances Stead Sellers, "Judge Rules New York County Can't Ban Unvaccinated Children from Schools, Parks," *Washington Post*, April 6, 2019. www.washingtonpost.com/national/judge-rules-new-york-county-cant-ban-unvaccinated-children-from-schools-parks/2019/04/06/589ae326-587e-11e9-8ef3-fbd41a2ce4d5.

The Difference Between "Live" and "Killed" Vaccines

There are two types of vaccines: "live" and "killed," or inactive, vaccines. Live vaccines use a weakened version of the disease, which can trigger an immune response without causing an actual infection. The medical term for this weakened version is "attenuated." Inactive vaccines use a killed version of the germ to prompt the immune system, though this immunity will not last as long as the immunity created by a live vaccine and may require additional booster shots to maintain lifelong immunity. Live vaccines currently recommended include the MMR vaccine, varicella (chickenpox), and rotavirus. Common inactive vaccines include Salk's polio vaccine and the seasonal influenza shot. The primary advantages of live vaccines is that they are relatively easy to produce and can often provide lifelong immunity. "Because a live, attenuated vaccine is the closest thing to a natural infection," explained the NIAID, "these vaccines are good 'teachers' of the immune system."[21] Live vaccines do mutate into potentially dangerous forms on rare occasions, though, and they are often not an option for people with weakened immune systems, such as people who have undergone chemotherapy for cancer. Live vaccines also need to be refrigerated, which makes them tough to use in developing countries with limited access to refrigeration.

Inactive vaccines, in contrast, contain pathogens that have been killed by exposure to heat, radiation, or various chemicals. Inactive vaccines are not as effective as live vaccines, but they do not require refrigeration, so they are frequently used in developing countries where electricity is unreliable.

The fact that inactive vaccines are made by exposure to chemicals makes some people nervous because it is not generally recommended for humans to come into contact with some of the chemicals used in vaccines. For example, formaldehyde is sometimes used to kill a pathogen for use in a vaccine, but formaldehyde is better known as an important chemical in the process of embalming, or preserving, a dead body. However, medical experts stress that only trace, or tiny, amounts remain in the final vaccine. According to the HHS, there is actually more formaldehyde found naturally in a living human body than there is in vaccines made with formaldehyde. When it comes to chemicals, the amount, application, and method by which they are put into the body determine whether or not they are

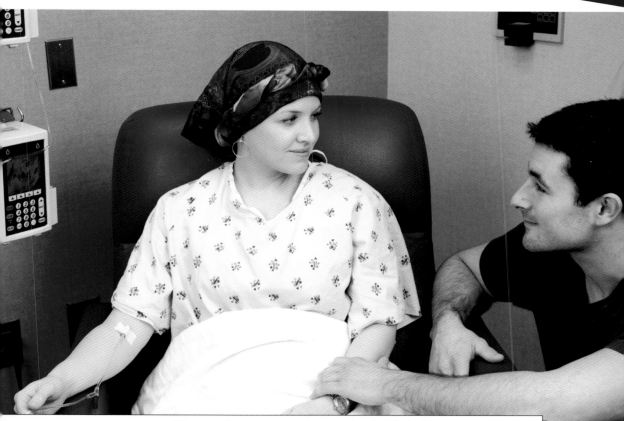

Chemotherapy weakens the body's immune system, making it harder for people to fight off other diseases—even the weakened version in vaccines.

harmful. It is important for people to understand the science and facts and ignore exaggerated statements that are frequently circulated on social media websites. Just about anything can be harmful to humans when it is taken into the body in an improper way or at too high an amount—for instance, water is essential in keeping people alive, but someone can die by drowning if they breathe it in instead of drinking it, or if they drink too much of it too quickly.

Within the killed and live categories, scientists have created vaccines to treat both bacterium- and virus-based infectious diseases. Therefore, there are four main classifications of vaccines: live-virus vaccines; killed-virus vaccines; subunit, recombinant, polysaccharide, and conjugate vaccines; and toxoid vaccines.

The best-known live-virus vaccines include the ones against measles, mumps, rotavirus, rubella, and smallpox. Albert Sabin's oral polio vaccine is one of the most famous examples of a live-virus vaccine.

A Closer Look

According to the Oxford Vaccine Group, a list of vaccine ingredients will generally include chemicals used to make the vaccine even if they do not remain in the finished vaccine.

The most famous killed-virus vaccine was Salk's polio vaccine. These types of vaccines were common in the early decades of vaccination. Other examples of inactive vaccines include those for hepatitis A and rabies. Live-virus versions are regarded as more effective in providing lifetime immunity against most diseases because, unlike killed-virus vaccines, they generally do not require booster shots.

Subunit, recombinant, polysaccharide, and conjugate vaccines are meant to target specific parts of a germ, such as its protein, sugar, or casing. Because these types of vaccines have been created to target very specific parts of the microbe, they can trigger strong and effective immune responses, though some may require additional booster shots for continued immunity. Examples of these types of vaccines include those for hepatitis B, shingles, pertussis, and human papillomavirus (HPV).

The process of making recombinant subunit vaccines begins when a scientist inserts a gene—a unit of DNA that plays a role in determining the characteristics an organism will have—that has been coded for a vaccine protein into either another "carrier" virus or cells that are being grown in a laboratory. When the carrier virus reproduces or when the cell metabolizes the protein, a new vaccine protein is created.

Conjugate vaccines are similar to recombinant vaccines in that they are made when scientists mix two different components together. Conjugate vaccines, though, are made by combining the outer coating of bacteria with a carrier protein. These complex vaccines are frequently used for infants and small children whose immune systems have not fully developed yet.

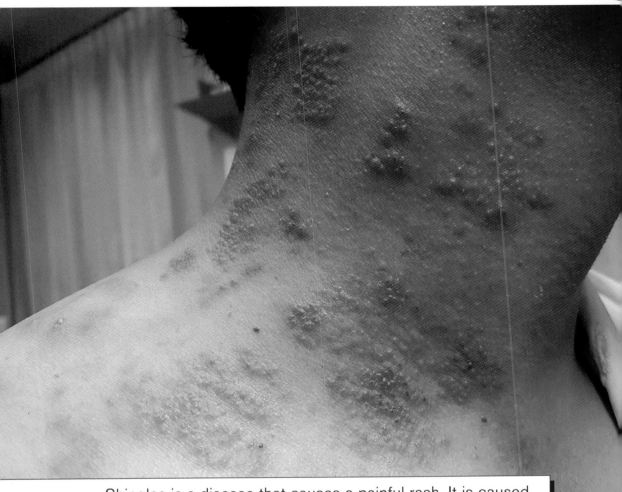

Shingles is a disease that causes a painful rash. It is caused by the varicella virus, which also causes chickenpox. Once someone has had chickenpox, the varicella virus hides in the body and can potentially return as shingles later in life. People who have never had chickenpox cannot catch shingles, but those who have not received the varicella vaccine can catch chickenpox from someone who has shingles.

The best-known vaccine that has been made using this technology is the one for *Haemophilus influenza* type b, also known as Hib disease. This disease was once the leading cause of bacterial meningitis in the United States for children under the age of five. Meningitis is an infection of the spinal cord and brain that can lead to brain damage, deafness, and other serious health problems. Before the development of the Hib vaccine, about 20,000 children contracted the disease every year. By 2015, thanks to the vaccine, the incidence of invasive Hib disease in the United States had dropped to 0.08 cases per 100,000 in children under the age of five, according to the CDC.

Toxoid vaccines are slightly different than other types of vaccines. Some bacterial diseases, such as tetanus and diphtheria, are not caused by bacteria themselves, but by the harmful chemicals—known as toxins—that those bacteria produce. Scientists took note of this important distinction, and they have figured out how to produce vaccines that neutralize these toxins. In essence, they create harmless "toxoid" versions of the dangerous toxin; these toxoids then trigger an immune system response. Once the immune system has created antibodies to defend against the toxoid material, those antibodies will also block the toxin if it appears. "Toxoids can actually be considered killed or inactivated vaccines, but are sometimes given their own category to highlight the fact that they contain an inactivated toxin, and not an inactivated form of bacteria,"[22] explained the History of Vaccines website, which is a project of the College of Physicians of Philadelphia.

Although each vaccine is developed to prevent a particular disease, a recent study suggests there could be additional, unintended benefits of vaccination. The study, published in the journal *Science Advances*, looked at the typhoid vaccine, which uses a weakened strain of salmonella. The researchers found that in addition to protecting against typhoid fever, the vaccine could help the body fight off other illnesses, such as the flu and yeast infections. Similar unexpected benefits have been seen in relation to other vaccinations, including the measles vaccine, which has been shown to reduce deaths from pneumonia and diarrhea as well as measles. Experts say that this reinforces the benefits of giving children vaccinations.

It is unclear exactly how a vaccine that is meant to target one illness could offer protection against a different illness. One possible explanation is that the live-virus vaccine trains other cells to fight off invading diseases. Dr. Michael Mina, a pathologist at the Harvard T.H. Chan School of Public Health, explained, "It would be like sending them to boot camp, making them ready to fight a new pathogen when it shows up."[23] Additional research is needed to test this theory, however, and identify how these unintended vaccination benefits appear.

A toxin is a poison that comes from a living organism. Small amounts cause disease, while larger amounts are frequently deadly. Snake venom is an example of a material that contains toxins.

The Future of Immunization

Historically, vaccines have turned disease-causing germs against the disease itself by triggering the body's immune response. However, researchers are continually evolving the science around immunization and searching for new ways to combat disease. One potential path scientists are studying is DNA vaccines. The idea behind DNA vaccines is that injecting a small bit of a virus's genetic code would prompt the body to produce the target viral protein—and, therefore, an immune response against it—without an actual infection. In this way, scientists believe that they may one day be able to turn the body's own cells into "vaccine-making factories, creating the antigens necessary to stimulate the immune system."[24]

Vaccine researchers hope this new technology will allow them to unlock effective forms of immunization for illnesses that continue to threaten humankind, such as tuberculosis and AIDS. There are several benefits to this type of vaccine: It produces a strong and effective immune response, the manufacturing process is easier, and it lasts longer because it does not require refrigeration. Currently, a number of DNA vaccines are in the early stages of clinical testing, including immunizations for hepatitis B and C as well as the Ebola and Zika viruses. However, none have yet been approved for human use by the FDA.

In addition to new types of vaccines, researchers are studying different ways to deliver immunizations in the hope of increasing vaccination rates; after all, most people do not enjoy getting shots. Some people choose not to get vaccines, such as the yearly flu shot, simply because they dislike needles. A couple of new forms of the influenza vaccine have had promising results. The live attenuated influenza vaccine, which is delivered via nasal spray, is now a recommended option to prevent flu infection. Although the nasal spray vaccine is not advised for people with certain chronic conditions such as asthma, children under the age of 2, people who are pregnant, or adults over the age of 50, the CDC states that the protection offered by the nasal spray is equal to that of a traditional injection.

In addition to the nasal spray option, researchers have been testing a pain-free microneedle patch for flu vaccination. The patch consists of 100 tiny needles that are just long enough to penetrate the skin. The needles contain the flu vaccine and dissolve into the skin in minutes. A 2017 study led by doctors Nadine Rouphael and Mark Mulligan of Emory University School of Medicine and Mark Prausnitz of the Georgia Institute of Technology found the patch to be safe and as effective as the traditional injection. "This bandage-strip sized patch of painless and dissolvable needles can transform how we get vaccinated," said Dr. Roderic I. Pettigrew, the director of the National Institute of Biomedical Imaging and Bioengineering (NIBIB). "A particularly attractive feature is that this vaccination patch could be delivered in the mail and self-administered. In addition, this technology holds promise for delivering other vaccines in the future."[25]

Larger clinical studies are needed, however, before consumers can expect this option to be available to them.

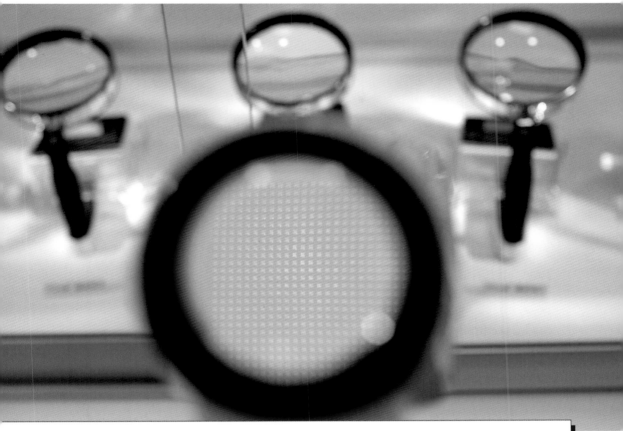

Shown here is a magnification of the experimental microneedle patch.

Unlike shots by syringe, which have to be delivered by a trained medical professional for safety reasons, both patch and nasal applications could be given by parents or other people without any special training. Supporters of this research say that either method of immunization would make it easier to vaccinate people in areas that are far from a doctor's office or in developing countries where trained doctors, nurses, and other medical personnel are rare.

Finally, researchers point out that many of the world's worst contagious diseases are now concentrated in developing countries, many of which have tropical or desert climates. This situation has led scientists to devote

New Health Risks from Climate Change

As the earth's climate continues to change dramatically, the risk of various diseases increases as well. Longer rainy seasons, for instance, have led to an increased number of mosquitoes, which thrive in warm, wet conditions. This, in turn, has caused a rise in mosquito-borne illnesses, including dengue fever, chikungunya, and malaria.

Prior to the 1970s, fewer than 10 countries had seen epidemics of dengue fever, a potentially deadly viral disease. However, an estimated 3.9 billion people across 128 different countries are now at risk of infection. In 2015, 2.35 million cases of the disease were reported in the Americas alone; of those, 10,200 cases were diagnosed as severe. These severe cases resulted in 1,181 deaths, according to WHO.

Dengvaxia, the first dengue vaccine to be developed, targets all four strains of the disease. It has been licensed in 20 countries, but as of 2019, it is only available in half of them. Clinical trials of the vaccine showed that children who previously had been infected by dengue were protected by the vaccine from getting the disease again. However, the vaccine proved to be more dangerous for children who had never contracted the disease before. Because of this increased risk, an expert panel advised WHO that the vaccine should only be given to people who are known to have had a previous dengue infection. As of April 2019, the FDA had not approved the vaccine for use within the mainland United States or its offshore territories, which include Puerto Rico, the U.S. Virgin Islands, and Guam.

As the risks of dangerous diseases continue to grow along with climate change, scientists are racing to find effective preventive measures and treatments. However, there are limits to how fast they can go since it will be important that any proposed vaccine be thoroughly tested for safety before it is distributed to vulnerable populations.

growing attention to developing vaccines that do not require storage in cold temperatures. In the meantime, some international health organizations have tried to overcome this obstacle by paying for refrigerated storage units for hospitals, trucks, cargo planes, and other transport vehicles in these parts of the world.

Chapter Three

GLOBAL TRENDS IN INFECTIOUS DISEASES

Vaccines have improved the lives of many throughout the developed world, helping to reduce the rate of infections diseases and, in some cases, fully eradicate some potentially deadly diseases. In fact, the U.S. government decided to stop mandatory smallpox vaccinations in 1972 because the virus had disappeared and was no longer considered a threat.

These trends are cause for celebration among doctors, scientists, public health officials, and parents around the world. They do not mean, however, that the risk of contracting other diseases has completely disappeared. Authorities say that children and adults who remain unvaccinated or fail to get booster shots are still vulnerable to a wide range of infectious diseases. Infants who are not yet old enough to receive their shots can still contract diseases as well.

Some diseases, in fact, are making comebacks. For example, annual cases of pertussis have risen steadily since the 1980s in the United States, peaking in 2012, when 48,277 cases were reported. Researchers believe this increase is related in large part to growing numbers of people who have never been vaccinated against the disease or have failed to get their pertussis booster shots. Another factor is the increased popularity of a new pertussis vaccine. Before 1997, children received a form of pertussis vaccine known as whole cell, which sometimes caused side effects that were more severe than other vaccines, such as convulsions (uncontrollable shaking of the body) and severe fevers. Since then, children have received the acellular version, which has fewer side effects but does not provide long-lasting immunity. People who were in high school as of 2019 were some of the first to receive the newer form of the vaccine, so the immunity issue has only recently been discovered.

The waning, or decreasing, immunity is problematic because it can lead to outbreaks of the illness, as happened in 2019 at a Los Angeles-area middle school, where 46 of the 1,600 students contracted pertussis even though all of the infected had been previously immunized. According to the *Los Angeles Times*, California law requires children to receive all of their doses of pertussis vaccine to be allowed to attend school, including the DTaP booster, unless they have a medical reason not to be vaccinated such as an allergy to the vaccine or a compromised immune system. However, the immunity granted by the middle school booster shot does not last long, according to a study by the Kaiser Permanente Vaccine Study Center.

Officials are divided about the best way to combat this waning immunity and prevent future outbreaks. Dr. Nicola P. Klein, the lead researcher of the Kaiser study, suggested officials switch from an age-based vaccination schedule to a more targeted approach, providing booster shots to kids before an outbreak is expected. However, Dr. Armand Dorian, chief medical officer at USC Verdugo Hills Hospital, believes it is too hard to predict outbreaks. He suggested focusing on increasing the vaccination rate, particularly among pregnant individuals, to prevent the bacteria from entering a community in the first place. "Once there's a chink [gap] in the armor and that unvaccinated population grows, then the actual protection of the vaccination significantly drops, even for those who are vaccinated,"[26] Dorian explained.

A Closer Look

A 2019 study that analyzed data from the flu seasons between 2012 and 2015 found no evidence of increased miscarriage risk for pregnant individuals after flu vaccination. The CDC recommends that all healthy adults, including people who are pregnant, get vaccinated for the flu.

Global Trends in Vaccine-Preventable Disease

Thanks to successful immunization campaigns, many terrible diseases have been fully or nearly eliminated throughout the United States. Some diseases, however, continue to be common, and a few illnesses that had previously been knocked down to historic lows are starting to crop up again due to dropping vaccination rates and increased travel. Around the globe, meanwhile, certain vaccine-preventable infectious diseases continue to wreak havoc on vulnerable populations.

Before a vaccine became available in 1995, virtually every kid in the United States got varicella—more commonly known as chickenpox. This was generally viewed as no worse than any other childhood illness since symptoms in most cases did not amount to more than a fever and an extremely itchy rash. In some serious cases, though, it could also cause skin infections and a condition called encephalitis, in which the brain swells dangerously. Since the introduction of the chickenpox vaccine in the United States, the annual number of chickenpox cases has dropped from about 4 million in the pre-vaccine era to fewer than 350,000 today.

In recent years, some parents have decided to expose their children to the virus through what they call "chickenpox parties" instead of getting them vaccinated. The idea is that when one child gets chickenpox, their parents advertise it and encourage others to bring their children over to "get it over with" and gain immunity naturally. Chickenpox parties were common before the vaccine was available; according to pediatrician Edith Bracho-Sanchez, the parties "were an OK idea in the days when parents had no other way to build long-lasting immunity in their children."[27] Chickenpox is often less severe in children than in adults, so at the time, it was better for someone to catch it when they were young. However, today, the vaccine can provide immunity with far less risk. Furthermore, it can protect others in addition to the vaccinated individual. The CDC states that the vaccine is not recommended for pregnant people and babies under the age of 1 year, so it is important for everyone who is eligible to be vaccinated to prevent the spread of the illness to these vulnerable individuals.

Chickenpox remains common in other parts of the world as well, especially in regions with a tropical climate. Refugee camps in countries such as Bangladesh are particularly vulnerable to outbreaks of this highly contagious virus. Dr. Mohammad Ahsanul Kabir, who runs a small health clinic in the Kutupalong refugee camps of Bangladesh, said he saw hundreds of cases in the first few months of 2019 alone. A report by NPR explained, "In late February … he was getting 30 to 35 cases a day just in his small, single-doctor clinic. By the end of March, there were nearly 65,000 reported throughout the sprawling Rohingya refugee camps."[28] Kabir explained

In refugee camps such as this one, diseases can spread quickly because so many people—most of whom do not have access to vaccines—are living so close together.

that the Rohingya people, who have fled a bloody war in Myanmar, did not have access to the basic childhood vaccinations recommended by WHO, which left them particularly vulnerable. While the virus typically clears up within a week for children, the real danger is for the unvaccinated adults in the refugee camps, in whom the infection can last up to a month and cause a more severe reaction. The Bangladesh Ministry of Health and various international aid organizations are working together to combat the spread of infectious disease in the camps, launching vaccination drives to try to get Rohingya kids immunized against a number of vaccine-preventable diseases, including diphtheria, tetanus, whooping cough, hepatitis B, and Hib.

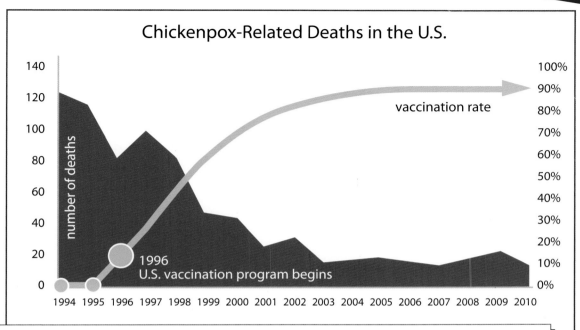

Chickenpox-Related Deaths in the U.S.

1996
U.S. vaccination program begins

vaccination rate

number of deaths

The U.S. chickenpox vaccination program has dramatically decreased the number of deaths caused by the disease, as this information from the CDC shows.

Another disease that is still a danger outside the United States is diphtheria, a bacterial infection that attacks the respiratory tract. It was once a deadly threat to American children. In the 1920s, in fact, diphtheria outbreaks infected an estimated 100,000 to 200,000 people per year, and annual deaths from the disease sometimes exceeded 15,000. Vaccination programs have played a vital role in beating back this disease over the years, though, and cases of diphtheria in the United States are now very rare. In fact, fewer than 5 cases were reported to the CDC in the past 10 years. It remains a serious problem in other parts of the world, however. In 2016, various countries reported about 7,100 cases of diphtheria to WHO, but there are likely many more cases that have gone unreported.

Hepatitis A is a virus that can cause serious and even fatal liver disease. It is generally spread through contact with fecal matter. According to the CDC, there were nearly 57,000 reported cases of hepatitis A in the United States in 1970—a rate of about 28 cases per 100,000 people. Twenty years later, the CDC reported nearly 31,500 cases—about

How Effective Are Vaccines?

Some people believe they should not bother getting vaccinated because sometimes people who are immunized against a certain disease still end up getting it. People who hold this view often point out that many people who get certain diseases in the United States have already received their vaccine for that disease, and that therefore, vaccines are useless at best and harmful at worst. However, WHO addressed these concerns by pointing out two important facts. First, no medication—including vaccines—is 100 percent effective. Everyone's body is different, and for a small number of people, certain medications are simply not as effective. According to WHO, vaccines are effective for 85 to 95 percent of people who get them. Second, the reason why most people who get certain diseases have been vaccinated is because there are simply more vaccinated than unvaccinated people in the United States. The organization gave a hypothetical example to help people understand:

> "In a high school of 1,000 students, none has ever had measles. All but five of the students ... are fully immunized [against measles]. The entire student body is exposed to measles, and every susceptible student becomes infected. The five unvaccinated students will be infected, of course. But ... in this class, seven students do not respond [to the vaccine], and they, too, become infected."

> As you can see, this doesn't prove the vaccine didn't work—only that most of the children in the class had been vaccinated, so those who were vaccinated and did not respond outnumbered those who had not been vaccinated. Looking at it another way, 100% of the children who had not been vaccinated got measles, compared with less than 1% of those who had been vaccinated.[1]

1. "Six Common Misconceptions About Immunization: 'The Majority of People Who Get Disease Have Been Vaccinated,'" World Health Organization, accessed on April 26, 2019. www.who.int/vaccine_safety/initiative/detection/immunization_misconceptions/en/index2.html.

12.6 cases per 100,000 people. Since a vaccine for this virus became available in the United States in 1995, however, rates have dropped dramatically. In 2016, there were about 2,000 acute cases of hepatitis A in America, with 70 deaths attributed to the virus. An acute case of a disease means that it comes on suddenly and can be cured relatively quickly. In contrast, a chronic case of a disease comes on more slowly and stays with the person forever. While the symptoms may eventually go away, depending on the disease, a person with a chronic pathogenic disease will always carry that pathogen in their body and may experience a recurrence of symptoms later on.

Hepatitis B also causes liver damage, but this virus spreads through contact with blood and other bodily fluids. Some people never completely recover from this disease, and about 3,000 to 5,000 of these chronically infected individuals died each year in the pre-vaccine era. America began vaccinating children against the virus in 1991, and rates have declined drastically since then. It still poses a significant public health problem, however. The CDC estimated that there were almost 20,900 cases of acute hepatitis B in the United States in 2016, and between 850,000 and 2.2 million cases of chronic hepatitis B. Globally, approximately 257 million people have chronic hepatitis B, according to the CDC.

Haemophilus influenzae type b (Hib) is a virus that can cause meningitis, pneumonia, epiglottitis (a severe throat infection), and other dangerous health problems. The United States began using the Hib vaccine for children in 1987 and for infants in 1990. Since then, the annual incidence of invasive Hib disease in children under the age of 5 has decreased by 99 percent. In 2015, the incidence of invasive Hib disease was 0.08 cases per 100,000 in children under the age of 5, according to the CDC.

Worldwide, WHO estimated that Hib caused at least 8.13 million cases of serious disease in 2000, and around 370,000 deaths of young children. Since that time, the virus has been brought under control in many wealthy, industrialized countries where the Hib vaccine has been added to standard immunization schedules. Its incidence has been dramatically reduced in some parts of the developing world as well. According to WHO, the Hib vaccine was introduced in 191 countries by the end of 2017, and global coverage with 3 doses of Hib vaccine was estimated at 72 percent.

Measles is a highly contagious disease that can cause deafness, blindness, encephalitis, and death. According to the CDC, prior to the

In the 21st century, many children started getting diseases that had previously been rare, such as measles. Being near them is dangerous to people who cannot get the vaccine.

introduction of the measles vaccine in 1963, an estimated 3 to 4 million people got measles each year in the United States, hundreds of whom died. The disease was declared eliminated in the United States in the year 2000, but outbreaks have become common in recent years due to lower vaccination rates and an increase in travel abroad. There were 17 measles outbreaks in 2018, which were mostly attributed to travelers bringing the illness home from abroad. This trend appeared to be continuing in 2019, as 1,095 cases of the disease throughout 28 states were reported to the CDC between January 1 and June 27, 2019.

For people who cannot get the vaccine, this is frightening and can negatively affect their lives even if they do not catch measles. For example, the vaccine is not recommended for children who are less than one year old, so parents of young children may end up avoiding public areas and changing travel plans to protect their kids from exposure.

Globally, measles deaths have decreased by 84 percent in recent years, from 550,100 in 2000 to 89,780 in 2016. However, the virus is still common in many developing countries, especially in parts of Africa and Asia. An estimated 7 million people were affected by measles in 2016, according to WHO.

Mumps, like chickenpox, is often seen as one of the milder infectious diseases that can affect children, but it can still lead to serious health problems such as meningitis, encephalitis, or deafness in rare cases. In addition, it is very unpleasant for the infected individual because the disease makes the glands that produce saliva swell. This makes just about any action, including swallowing, extremely painful.

Mumps occurs worldwide, but it is fairly rare in the United States. Vaccination against mumps in the United States began in 1967, and its effectiveness in combating the disease quickly became evident. U.S. mumps cases have decreased more than 99 percent since then, with only a few hundred cases reported most years. However, since 2006, there have been several increases in cases and outbreaks, mainly due to decreasing rates of vaccination. Between January 2016 and June 2017, for example, 150 outbreaks resulting in 9,200 individual cases were reported by health officials. The largest outbreak occurred in a close-knit community in northwest Arkansas, resulting in nearly 3,000 cases. As of June 2019, more than 1,400 cases have been reported to the CDC from 44 different states.

Pertussis remains a feared childhood disease around the world. It is highly contagious—even people who are fully immunized can sometimes catch it—and its symptoms can be life-threatening for children. Cases of pertussis can result in pneumonia, seizures, and brain infections.

According to a 2017 study, there are about 24.1 million cases of pertussis per year worldwide and about 160,700 deaths in children under the age of five.

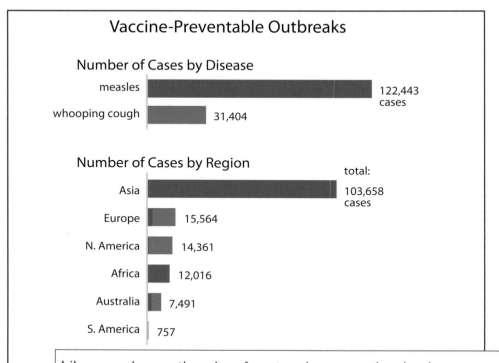

Vaccine-Preventable Outbreaks

Number of Cases by Disease

- measles — 122,443 cases
- whooping cough — 31,404

Number of Cases by Region

total:

- Asia — 103,658 cases
- Europe — 15,564
- N. America — 14,361
- Africa — 12,016
- Australia — 7,491
- S. America — 757

Like measles, outbreaks of pertussis are on the rise in the United States and other countries despite the wide availability of a vaccine, as this 2014 information from the Council on Foreign Relations shows.

The disease is less of a threat in the United States, but flare-ups do occur on a regular basis. Scientists also report that pertussis rates are rising in the United States due to decreasing rates of vaccination. In 2000, for example, the CDC reported 7,867 cases of pertussis in the United States. Ten years later, 27,550 cases of pertussis were reported to the CDC. In both instances, however, the CDC believes that the actual number of cases was higher than reported. In 2012, the most recent peak year, the CDC reported 48,277 cases of pertussis in the United States, the largest number of reported cases since 1955.

Pneumococcal disease is caused by different strains of bacteria that attack various parts of the body. Pneumococcal pneumonia attacks the lungs, for example, while pneumococcus bacteria can also cause meningitis. Another common form of pneumococcal disease causes a condition called bacteremia, which is an infection of the blood. According to the CDC, about 900,000 Americans get pneumococcal pneumonia each year; the organization reported an estimated 3,700 deaths from pneumococcal meningitis and bacteremia in 2013. The National Foundation for Infectious Disease also reported that there are an estimated 175,000 hospitalized cases of pneumococcal pneumonia, 34,500 cases of bacteremia, and 2,200 cases of meningitis each year in the United States. Different vaccines are available for elderly people and infants, but public health authorities say that about one-third of Americans over the age of 65 have never been vaccinated against this disease.

Polio has been eradicated in the United States, and while it is still present in certain other countries, experts believe vaccination will eventually wipe it out all over the world. In 1999, WHO reported:

> Mass immunization campaigns which reach hundreds of millions of children in a few days have had a dramatic impact on the disease. Children have been reached in some of the remotest corners of the world. Health workers have used camels, horses, dug-out canoes, boats and motor-bikes to get the vaccines through. In many countries polio immunization campaigns have been used to deliver vitamin A supplements as well, increasing the impact of immunization on child health.[29]

Today, experts agree that these mass immunization efforts have pushed polio to the brink of extinction. In 2019, WHO reported that polio cases had decreased by more than 90 percent since 1988, from an estimated 350,000 in more than 125 countries to just 33 reported cases in 2018. The organization also reported that for the first time in its history, India—the second-most populous nation in the world—did not record a single case of polio for a one-year period (from early 2011 to early 2012). This announcement was all the more remarkable considering that as recently as 2009, India had more cases of polio than any other nation in the world.

Rotavirus infections can trigger severe bouts of vomiting and diarrhea in small children. Prior to the development of a vaccine, this highly contagious virus accounted for the hospitalization of 50,000 to 70,000 children annually—and about 20 to 60 deaths—in the United States. Two rotavirus vaccines were developed and approved for use in the United States in 2006 and 2008, and these medicines have already begun to reduce rotavirus infections in America. According to the CDC, the vaccine prevents an estimated 40,000 to 50,000 hospitalizations among U.S. infants and young children per year.

Immunization programs for rotavirus are also being put in place in developing countries, where the disease is far more common. Rotavirus is transmitted via fecal matter, which often gets into the water or food supply in countries with poor sanitation. According to PATH, rotavirus causes about one-third of child deaths due to diarrhea, with 215,000 deaths recorded worldwide in 2013.

Rubella only causes mild rash and fever symptoms in most cases, but it poses a grave danger to pregnant people and their unborn children. "If a pregnant woman gets rubella," reported the CDC, "her unborn baby has about an 80 percent chance of 'congenital rubella syndrome' (CRS), which can lead to deafness, blindness, mental impairment, or heart or brain damage."[30]

After being introduced in 1969, the rubella vaccine greatly reduced the toll of this disease. In fact, WHO announced in 2015 that the Americas are the world's first region to eliminate rubella and CRS. However, people can contract the disease elsewhere in the world and bring it into the region, so vaccination remains an important preventive action.

Tetanus, which is sometimes also called lockjaw, is unlike most other infectious diseases in that it does not pass from person to person. It is contracted through a cut or wound that becomes contaminated with tetanus bacteria, which can be found in soil, dust, and manure. The bacteria

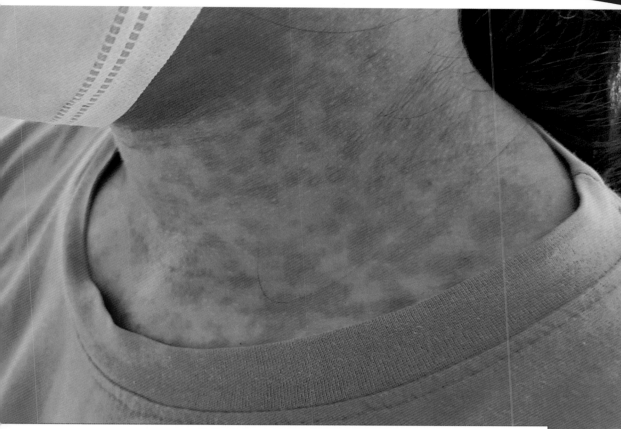

Rubella (shown here) can pose a serious danger to pregnant women. The disease is sometimes called German measles because the first scientists to identify rubella and write a detailed description of its symptoms were German.

then attack the nervous system, where they can cause such severe muscle spasms that the infected person's jaw becomes "locked," meaning it is difficult to open the mouth or swallow. Sometimes it can be deadly. Tetanus is very rare in the United States thanks to a well-established immunization program that includes booster shots every 10 years. The United States averages only about 30 cases of tetanus per year. Worldwide, WHO estimated that neonatal tetanus—in other words, tetanus contracted by newborns—killed about 49,000 children in 2013. While this number may seem high, it represents a 94 percent reduction from 1988, when an estimated 787,000 babies died of tetanus within their first month of life.

New vaccines are being invented and tested all the time, but coming up with a safe and effective new medication is often difficult. For example, until recently, there was no vaccine for malaria. Various pills exist to both prevent and treat malaria; one of the most common is called Malarone, and in the United States, it is most commonly prescribed to people who plan to travel to an area where malaria is common. Malarone is taken once a day for the entire trip, as well as two days before and one week after. However, for long trips, taking a large supply of Malarone can be expensive, and some people experience unpleasant side effects. Furthermore, it is not practical for people who live in countries where malaria is a constant threat.

A Closer Look

Unlike other pathogens, the parasite that causes malaria changes shape inside the body. This makes it very difficult for antibodies to consistently recognize what the parasite is.

In April 2019, a malaria vaccine called RTS,S was rolled out, and WHO committed to a vaccination campaign targeting children in several African countries, including Malawi, Ghana, and Kenya. Some people praised the campaign because it can give the children who receive it protection against a disease that kills about 1,200 people worldwide each day. However, others criticized it because the vaccine only works about 4 times out of 10 and requires 4 shots spread out over 18 months. It can be especially difficult for people in developing countries to travel to a doctor, so this may make it difficult for the campaign to complete its goal. Furthermore, some experts have noted that by the time RTS,S has finished clinical trials that are done to prove it is safe for humans, there will likely be other, more effective malaria vaccines on the market, so it is not necessary to commit to using RTS,S simply because it is the first. Some people have pointed out that vaccines that affect people in developing countries are slow to be put on the market, while those that help people in developed countries such as the United States tend to be put out more quickly. This, they speculate, is because people in developing countries have less money and therefore cannot often afford to pay for the drug. They accuse Big Pharma, or the pharmaceutical industry, of being more willing to help the rich than the poor. While many pharmaceutical companies deny this accusation, they have admitted that the process of developing new drugs is slow and not always efficient. Many companies are looking for newer, better ways to create new medications.

The Battle Against Infectious Disease Continues

With numerous outbreaks of potentially deadly diseases cropping up across the United States, a renewed emphasis on the safety and effectiveness of vaccines is imperative. In 2018, WHO's Strategy Group of Experts on Immunization released a report that illustrates the tenuous state of the war against infectious disease throughout the globe:

> Immunization has proven the test of time as one of public health's most cost-effective interventions. In 2017, the number of children immunized—116.2 million—was the highest ever reported. Since 2010, 113 countries have introduced new vaccines, and more than 20 million additional children have been vaccinated.
>
> Nevertheless, this year starkly illustrates how easily hard-won gains are lost. Because of low coverage nationally, or pockets of low coverage, multiple WHO regions have been hit with large measles and diphtheria outbreaks causing many deaths. The continued detection of circulating vaccine-derived poliovirus is further evidence that national immunization programmes are not achieving the goal of reaching every child.
>
> This picture provides a backdrop for discussions of the future of immunization after 2020. The immunization community must seek to maintain its hard-won gains but also aim to do more and to do things better. Immunization is a central pillar of universal health coverage.[31]

Chapter Four

AVAILABLE VACCINES

Many people think of vaccines as something children get, not teens or adults. In fact, most people do not know their immunization status. They may not realize they were never given all the recommended vaccines when they were young, or that the time has come for them to get their booster shots. Doctors' offices keep records of such things, but they may forget to remind patients about their immunizations, especially if they only see patients when they are sick—a bad time to give their immune system something else to fight off. It is important for patients to think about what vaccinations they might need and discuss this with their doctor when they go in for their regular check-up.

The Flu Shot

The flu is a highly contagious respiratory sickness caused by one of many influenza viruses. Although it is often confused with the common cold, the flu is typically worse than a cold and can cause serious and life-threatening complications, including pneumonia; inflammation of the heart, brain, or muscle tissues; and multi-organ failure. Children under the age of 5, pregnant people, and adults over the age of 65 are particularly at risk of developing serious flu-related complications. There are two main types of influenza virus: types A and B, which cause annual seasonal flu epidemics. These viruses are constantly changing due to genetic shifts that occur as the virus replicates. It is these genetic changes that make it possible for a person to get sick with the flu multiple times in their life: The body's immune system may not recognize the virus after changes have occurred.

Since the virus constantly changes, annual flu vaccinations are recommended for everyone over the age of 6 months by the end of each October.

Getting vaccinated later can still be beneficial, though, and vaccinations should remain available throughout the entire flu season. The vaccine, which is reviewed and updated as needed every year, has been a key part of preventing complications due to flu. For example, vaccination prevented approximately 7 million flu illnesses, 109,000 flu hospitalizations, and 8,000 flu deaths during the 2017–2018 flu season, according to the CDC.

In the United States, many places make it easy to get a flu shot by allowing people to come in without an appointment. Additionally, most kinds of health insurance cover the shot.

A common misconception about the flu vaccine is that it actually causes the flu. According to the CDC, the vaccine is made either with flu viruses that are inactive and are therefore not infectious or with only a single gene from a flu virus (as opposed to the full virus) in order to produce an

Why Did I Get the Flu After I Got My Flu Shot?

According to the CDC, there are a number of reasons why a vaccinated person would experience flu symptoms. These include:

1. *Other respiratory viruses besides flu such as rhinoviruses, which are associated with the common cold, cause symptoms similar to flu, and also spread and cause illness during the flu season. The flu vaccine only protects against influenza, not other illnesses ...*

2. *It is possible to be exposed to influenza viruses ... shortly before getting vaccinated or during the two-week period after vaccination that it takes the body to develop immune protection. This exposure may result in a person becoming ill with flu before protection from the vaccine takes effect ...*

3. *They may have been exposed to a flu virus that is very different from the viruses the vaccine is designed to protect against. The ability of a flu vaccine to protect a person depends largely on the similarity or "match" between the viruses selected to make the vaccine and those spreading and causing illness ...*

4. *The flu vaccine can vary in how well it works and some people who get vaccinated may still get sick.*[1]

However, several studies have shown that vaccination can reduce the severity of illness in people who get vaccinated but still get sick. Additionally, getting vaccinated helps protect other people who are more vulnerable to serious flu illness, such as babies and young children, older people, and people with certain chronic health conditions.

1. "Misconceptions About Seasonal Flu and Flu Vaccines," CDC, last updated September 25, 2018. www.cdc.gov/flu/about/qa/misconceptions.htm.

immune response without causing infection. While it is true that some people experience side effects ranging from soreness and redness at the injection site to low-grade fever, headache, and muscle aches, these symptoms typically clear up in a couple of days. "The most common reactions people have to flu vaccines are considerably less severe than the symptoms caused by actual flu illness,"[32] noted the CDC.

Flu infections are highly contagious and spread easily in schools, households, churches, childcare settings, and workplaces. They can also take a particularly heavy toll on children and adolescents. It is unsurprising, therefore, that family doctors and public health experts emphasize the importance of yearly flu shots. Since flu viruses change from year to year, vaccines are also updated to provide protection against the most recent flu strains. Some people believe they can avoid the flu simply by taking precautions such as washing their hands frequently and avoiding people who are sick, but people are generally contagious before they ever start showing symptoms. "A yearly influenza vaccine is the first and most important step an individual can take in protecting against the flu,"[33] confirmed Jeff Dimond of the CDC. The flu can also have more than just negative physical effects on someone; a survey by the drugstore chain Walgreens released in late 2011, for example, found that the 2010–2011 flu season resulted in a total of 100 million lost workdays, $7 billion in lost wages, and 32 million missed school days.

A Closer Look

When people suddenly come down with vomiting or diarrhea that clears up within a few days, they frequently refer to it as the "stomach flu." However, this illness is not caused by the influenza virus, so the flu shot does not protect against it. Most commonly, sudden-onset, short-term vomiting and diarrhea is the result of norovirus—a common cause of food poisoning—although there can be other causes as well.

Government health care experts and physicians note that flu viruses change over time. Most years, however, scientists are able to adjust flu

A Young Life Cut Short by the Flu

Many people believe the flu is nothing serious, so many choose not to get their yearly flu shot. However, the story of a girl named Britt shows that this is not always true. Britt's infection with influenza A started with a sore throat, but quickly escalated. The National Foundation for Infectious Diseases reported in 2017:

> On March 24, 2016, Britt complained that her throat was itchy, so she picked up some over-the-counter medicine. Later that evening, she seemed to be feeling better although her voice was a little raspy. The next morning, Britt told her mother that she wasn't feeling quite like herself. Her mother gave her some toast and juice and then helped Britt to bed. Fifteen minutes later, Britt's mother went to check on her and Britt indicated that she was feeling okay.
>
> Later that day, around 11:45 AM, Britt's mother heard a weird sound coming from her room and as she entered Britt's room, she found her lying still, on her back. She tried to wake Britt but she was unresponsive, so she called 911. When the ambulance arrived, Britt had no pulse. The paramedics immediately rushed her to the hospital ...
>
> Upon arrival, the medical staff told Britt's mother that her condition was not stabilizing despite attempts to treat her blood pressure and oxygen levels. The medical staff indicated that Britt was experiencing sepsis and explained to her mother that she should be prepared to make a medical decision concerning Britt's life.
>
> On the morning of March 26, 2016, Britt went into cardiac arrest twice within a few minutes and her mother made the difficult decision to stop life-saving efforts.[1]

1. "Brittany's Story: A Young Life Lost to Influenza," NFID, December 7, 2017. nfid.wordpress.com/2017/12/07/brittanys-story-a-young-life-lost-to-influenza/.

vaccines so they immunize people against the viruses circulating at that time. In 2009, for example, Americans looking for protection from ordinary flu as well as the pandemic H1N1 strain, which was wreaking havoc across the Americas at the time, had to take two different shots. Beginning in 2010 and every year since, however, vaccine makers adjusted the product so that their regular flu vaccine included immunization against H1N1. This is why research into diseases and vaccines is so crucial: Without studying virus trends, vaccine makers would never be able to come up with an effective formula in time to immunize people each year.

Current Recommended Vaccines

Fortunately, most people today have never seen the devastating consequences vaccine-preventable diseases can have on a child, family, or community. Although these diseases may not be common in the United States, they do persist around the world, so it is important to continue protecting children in the Americas and elsewhere with vaccines. As evidenced by recent outbreaks of vaccine-preventable diseases such as pertussis and measles, these diseases always have the potential to crop up.

Some people believe the current vaccination schedule is too much for children's bodies to handle. However, according to experts such as pediatrician and vaccine researcher Paul Offit,

> When a baby's in the womb, they're in a sterile environment. But when they enter the birth canal and then enter the world, they're not. And very quickly they have—living on the surface of their bodies, their nose, their throat, their intestine, their skin—they have literally trillions of bacteria ... you have trillions of bacteria [that] live on your body, to which you make an immune response. Each single bacterium has between 2,000 and 6,000 immunological components. The total number of immunological components contained in all ... vaccines that children get in the first few years of life is 150 ... that [is] literally a drop in the ocean of what children encounter and manage every day.[34]

The CDC currently recommends that all healthy infants receive 10 vaccines in the first two years of life, which help protect against 14 different diseases. Each one has its own schedule that has been designed to provide the most effective protection.

Sometimes people come into contact with dangerous objects even if they are not doing a risky activity at the time. In particular, nails can often be found in unexpected places. Someone who receives a puncture wound from a nail that is rusty generally needs a tetanus shot.

The DTaP vaccine protects against diphtheria, tetanus, and pertussis in a single shot. The vaccine needs to be given a total of five times for full immunity. The recommended schedule for these shots for children is at the ages of 2 months, 4 months, 6 months, 15 to 18 months, and 4 to 6 years (before the child enters school). In addition, scientists have developed related vaccines for older patients. Td vaccine is a tetanus-diphtheria vaccine given to teens and adults as a booster shot every 10 years or sometimes after an exposure to tetanus; for example, someone whose foot gets punctured after they step on a rusty nail may need a tetanus booster even if they are up to date with their Td vaccine. Tdap vaccine, meanwhile, also provides extended protection against pertussis. Doctors recommend a single dose of Tdap for adolescents in the range of 11 to 18 years and adults in the range of 19 to 64 years.

MMR vaccine protects against measles, mumps, and rubella in a single shot. The vaccine needs to be given twice for full protection. Doctors recommend that children receive this vaccine at 12 to 15 months old, and then again at 4 to 6 years old.

Varicella vaccine protects against chickenpox. The vaccine needs to be given twice for full protection. Doctors recommend that children receive this vaccine at 12 to 15 months old, and

Special Vaccines

Some vaccines are not necessary for the general public but are highly recommended for certain groups. For example, people who live in the United States do not need to get vaccinated against yellow fever because the virus exists almost exclusively in tropical and subtropical areas of Africa and South America. Visitors to these areas are highly encouraged to get the vaccine before they go because there is no cure for it. Some people recover from the disease on their own, but for up to 50 percent of infected people, it is deadly. Yellow fever is spread mainly through the bites of infected mosquitoes; it is not transmitted through person-to-person contact, so even if an infected traveler returns to the United States, they cannot infect those around them. However, if a mosquito bites them, that mosquito can then potentially spread the virus to other people by biting them. Because yellow fever and other travel vaccines—such as cholera, typhoid, and Japanese encephalitis—are not regularly recommended for American citizens, they are generally only available at special travel clinics and may not be covered by health insurance.

People in the military also get vaccines that the general public does not. This is because they are put in more dangerous situations than the average citizen. For example, the U.S. government has concerns about the smallpox virus being weaponized by enemies and used to infect people as an act of war. Military personnel would likely be the first ones infected in this case. Since smallpox has been declared eradicated, it is unnecessary for most people to be vaccinated; furthermore, this vaccine is one of the few that is known to commonly cause dangerous side effects, so for the vast majority of people, the risks of getting it far outweigh the benefits. Another vaccine only recommended for soldiers is the one for anthrax, a bacterial disease that is rare and not contagious. Again, most people will never come into contact with anthrax and therefore do not need a vaccine, but anthrax has been used as a weapon by terrorists. Anthrax vaccination is also recommended for some people who work with animals. The bacterium that causes anthrax is found in the soil and can be transmitted to animals that eat from infected areas; when people such as farm workers come into contact with an infected animal, they can then contract the disease.

then again at 4 to 6 years old. Recently, however, scientists have developed a single MMRV vaccine that combines the MMR and varicella treatments. Children who get the MMRV vaccine only have to get one shot instead of the two they would need if they took the separate MMR and varicella vaccines, but recipients of the MMRV vaccine are at slightly greater risk of developing a post-immunization fever or other temporary side effects.

HepA vaccine protects against hepatitis A. Approved for children who are at least 2 years old, it requires two doses that should be given at least six months apart.

HepB vaccine protects against hepatitis B. Unlike other vaccines, the first dose of HepB is given at birth. Two follow-up doses are typically given at 1 month and 6 months of age for full immunization. A two-dose version of this vaccine is also available for teenagers who do not get the immunization as infants.

Hib vaccine provides immunization against *Haemophilus influenzae* type b (Hib). The recommended childhood vaccination schedule for Hib is at 2 months, 4 months, 6 months, and 12 to 15 months of age. There is one brand of Hib vaccine that does not require the 6-month shot, but not all doctor's offices carry it.

The seasonal influenza vaccine is recommended for everyone over 6 months of age. Vaccine makers have developed three versions of the flu shot: one for young people 6 months to 18 years old, one for adults from 18 to 64 years old, and one for seniors who are 65 or older.

PCV13 vaccine protects against pneumococcal disease. The standard PCV13 vaccination schedule calls for four doses to be given to infants at 2 months, 4 months, 6 months, and 12 to 15 months. If vaccination is not given or completed during these early months of life, a single-dose version is also available for children ages 2 to 4.

Polio vaccine immunizes children against the poliomyelitis virus. The United States has used inactivated polio vaccine (IPV) since 2000, but many other parts of the world still use oral polio vaccine (OPV). Doctors recommend four doses of IPV for children, at 2 months, 4 months, 6 to 18 months, and 4 to 6 years old.

Rotavirus is the leading cause of severe diarrhea and vomiting illness among children around the world. This can lead to death by dehydration if fluids are not replaced quickly enough. American pediatricians and public health experts currently recommend that infants get one of

How to Talk to Parents About the HPV Vaccine

Some parents are hesitant to have their child vaccinated against HPV because they worry it might encourage early sexual activity. However, it is recommended by the AAP for all young adults, regardless of whether they are sexually active yet or not. The website DoSomething.org gives some tips for how young adults can talk to their parents about allowing them to get the vaccine. It includes questions a parent might ask and scripts for answering those questions. For example, if a parent asks if HPV is harmful enough to warrant a vaccine, their child can answer, "Yes! HPV is a major cause of cervical cancer and has been linked to other types of cancer … It can also cause genital warts. Also, people can pass the virus to others even if they don't show any symptoms."[1] Other scripts include answers to questions or comments such as:

- *"How common is HPV?"*

- *"I really don't feel comfortable having this conversation with you."*

- *"You're too young for sex, so you're too young for vaccination."*

- *"Is HPV vaccination even effective?"*

- *"Doesn't HPV only affect women?"*

- *"Can't you just get screened for cancers at your next doctors visit?"*

- *"What if we can't afford HPV vaccines?"*[2]

If someone ultimately feels too uncomfortable to talk to their parents about this issue, DoSomething.org has made cards that include a number parents can text for more information. A young adult can print one of the cards out and give it to their parents without further discussion.

1. Margot Harris and Mac Patrick, "How to Have 'The Talk' with Your Parents … About HPV Vaccination!," DoSomething.org, accessed on April 26, 2019. www.dosomething.org/us/the-talk-guide.

2. Harris and Patrick, "How to Have 'The Talk.'"

two types of rotavirus vaccine. The first vaccine calls for doses at 2 and 4 months of age, while the second vaccine type calls for a third dose at 6 months of age.

Many of these childhood vaccines can be delivered to patients at the same office visit. Doctors note, however, that vaccination guidelines vary for people of all ages who have other health issues. As of 2019, all of these vaccinations are traditionally delivered by injection except for the rotavirus vaccine, which is given orally. Some doctors may have other options available, such as the nasal spray that protects against influenza.

Vaccines for Tweens and Teens

The HPV vaccine is sometimes overlooked because parents frequently do not want to think about their child engaging in sexual activity. However, the reality is that about 40 percent of high school students report having had sexual intercourse. Furthermore, according to the CDC, half of the 20 million new sexually transmitted disease (STD) cases each year are reported by people between the ages of 15 and 24.

Gardasil, the first vaccine for HPV, was approved by the FDA in 2006 after clinical trials showed the vaccine was effective at preventing infection by four types of HPV. This made headline news, since HPV affects about 79 million Americans, most in their late teens and early 20s. A second form of the vaccine called Gardasil 9, which protects against nine strains of the virus, was approved by the FDA in 2014.

In nine out of ten cases, people who contract HPV get rid of the disease naturally within two years, generally without developing any symptoms or health problems from it. However, some strains of the virus can cause cervical and other cancers to develop, including cancer of the vulva, vagina, penis, anus, and back of the throat. The risk of getting cervical cancer from HPV is significant for people who have uteruses. The CDC estimates that about 10,000 people a year get cervical cancer, and in nearly all cases, their cancer comes from HPV infection. Approximately 33,700 people are affected each year by cancers caused by HPV.

In light of these health risks, most pediatricians and public health experts strongly encourage parents to immunize their children with the two-dose HPV vaccine at age 11 or 12. A three-dose HPV vaccine is recommended for teens and young adults who start the series later, between ages 15 and 26, as well as individuals with weakened immune systems between the ages of 9 and 26. The CDC says that these vaccines are safe and can prevent 90 percent—30,300 cases—of cancers caused by HPV from developing in the United States each year.

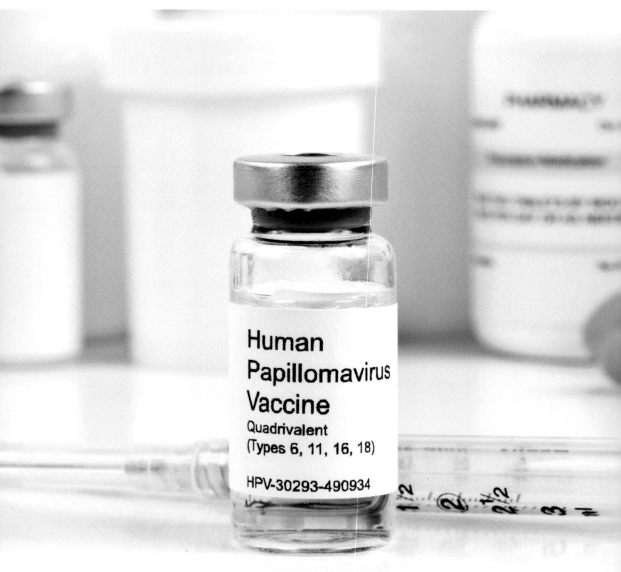

Thanks to the HPV vaccine, the rate of cervical cancer in young women has dropped dramatically even though the rate of sexual activity has remained the same.

Despite its effectiveness, the HPV vaccine has triggered criticism from some conservative parents, lawmakers, and policy analysts. They worry that vaccinating teens against an STD gives them permission to engage in sexual activity. Most physicians and public health experts—and many parents—disagree with this view. They point out that HPV vaccination is voluntary, and they emphasize that the whole point of the vaccine is to protect children from developing life-threatening forms of cancer in adulthood.

A Closer Look

Although the HPV vaccine provides long-lasting protection against HPV infection and disease, it does not protect against pregnancy or other sexually transmitted diseases, such as herpes and syphilis. The CDC recommends that sexually active individuals use condoms the proper way every time they engage in sex.

The vaccine has proven incredibly effective at reducing the cancer-causing virus. A decade after the vaccine was introduced, a study published in the journal *Pediatrics* showed a 64 percent drop in the rates of HPV among teens. Infectious disease specialist Dr. Joseph Bocchini told NPR at the time that he hoped the results would encourage doctors to make a stronger recommendation to parents to vaccinate their children before they become exposed to the virus. "We have a great opportunity at age 11 to 12 to vaccinate all boys and girls against a group of viruses that are important causes of cancer,"[35] he said. Although HPV is most commonly associated with cancers that affect female genitalia, Bocchini noted, "There are over 9,000 cases of HPV-associated cancer in males each year in the United States. Many of those cases are cancers of the mouth and throat. So it is very likely that we could see a significant drop in cases of cancer of the mouth and throat in both men and women with the use of HPV vaccines."[36] As of 2017, however, only 49 percent of adolescents between the ages of 13 and 17 in the United States had received the complete three-dose series of the HPV vaccine.

Sometimes wild animals get rabies. Some people believe that if a raccoon is outside in the daytime, that is a sure sign it has rabies, but animal experts say it is not unusual for raccoons to be active during the day. If the raccoon or other wild animal is acting unusual—for example, if it is walking oddly or lets someone get close enough to touch it—it is likely sick.

In addition to these immunizations that take place in the offices of pediatricians across the country, scientists have developed a variety of other vaccines that protect against other diseases. Some of these vaccines are only recommended for certain groups of people. Veterinarians and other people who regularly handle animals, for example, are encouraged to stay up to date on their rabies vaccines. In contrast, a person who does not regularly work with animals generally only needs a rabies vaccine if an animal bites them.

Chapter Five

GOING VIRAL

In 2016, Joshua Nerius, a 30-year-old resident of Chicago, Illinois, developed a high fever and a rash. He was prescribed antibiotics, but his health continued to deteriorate. Finally, Nerius went to the emergency room, where he was told his illness looked very much like measles. The doctor asked whether he had been vaccinated as a child. Nerius texted the question to his mother; she replied with a thumbs-down emoji.

To protect others from catching the disease from him, Nerius was placed in an isolation room at Northwestern Memorial Hospital. He became so weak that at one point, he could not walk without assistance. He lost 25 pounds and did not completely recover for several months. "I felt horrible," Nerius said in an interview with CNN. "It took a serious toll."[37]

When he considers recent outbreaks of vaccine-preventable illnesses and his own debilitating battle with measles, Nerius becomes frustrated. "It makes me so angry. My parents thought they were doing the right thing. They were persuaded by the anti-vaxers,"[38] he said. Anti-vaxers (also spelled anti-vaxxers) are people who promote the anti-vax, or anti-vaccination, movement for various reasons. Despite mounting scientific evidence disproving any supposed link between vaccination and the rising rates of autism and other developmental conditions, health officials struggle to combat continuing reluctance to protect children from vaccine-preventable diseases.

While scientists, doctors, and other health officials continue to emphasize the safety and effectiveness of vaccines, a growing number of Americans insist the dangers of vaccination are ignored or understated.

Opting Out of Vaccination

According to the National Conference of State Legislatures, all U.S. states have laws requiring certain vaccines for students, though all school immunization laws allow exemptions to children for medical reasons—for example, if they are allergic to an ingredient in a vaccine. Additionally, almost all states grant exemptions for people who have religious beliefs against immunizations. Currently, 17 states allow philosophical exemptions for those who object to immunizations because of personal, moral, or other similar beliefs. A 2018 study published in *PLOS Medicine* found that since 2009, the number of philosophical exemptions to vaccination has increased in two-thirds of the states that allow such exemptions, making these areas increasingly vulnerable to disease outbreaks.

Why Some People Fear Vaccines

There are many arguments that anti-vaccination supporters point to in order to appeal to parents, including a seemingly packed infant vaccination schedule, anecdotal (based on personal stories instead of research and facts) evidence of harm attributed to vaccines, a perceived rising rate of autism, and fears of too much government involvement in citizens' personal lives.

The overwhelming majority of pediatricians, scientists, and public health experts who work on disease-related issues insist that there is no basis for these fears. They freely admit that vaccines occasionally cause negative side effects. They emphasize, however, that studies have found no causal link between vaccination and autism or ADHD. Finally, supporters of vaccination remind people repeatedly that vaccines have greatly reduced the threat of illness or death from many frightening diseases.

Their assurances have not done much to relieve the concerns of parents who are skeptical of vaccines. In fact, a growing number of parents have decided against immunizing their children with some or all of the vaccines recommended by national health organizations. This trend has angered and frustrated many pediatricians and health care officials, but anti-vaxxers refuse to budge. This deadlock has created tension between the two camps. As journalist David Kirby wrote, "Each side accuses the other of

Shown here are demonstrators at the 2017 March for Science in Toronto, Canada, holding signs supporting vaccination.

being irrational, overzealous, blind to evidence they find inconvenient, and subject to professional, financial, or emotional conflicts of interest that cloud their judgment."[39]

The Study That Sparked the Autism Debate

The first rumblings of concern about a possible link between vaccines and rising rates of autism and other developmental disabilities were heard in

Fighting Misinformation Parent to Parent

In the age of social media, fake studies and scary stories can spread like wildfire within hours. To combat the spread of misinformation about vaccines, some peer-focused organizations are encouraging parents to get educated and share facts with other parents. Kim Nelson, a mother of two in South Carolina, counters so-called "fake news" by posting scientific articles online, responding to private messages from fellow parents who have questions about vaccines, and adding supportive comments to posts by other parents. "I very much believe if you have the ability to advocate, then you have to," she said. "The onus [responsibility] is on us if we want change."[1]

Timing is important when it comes to educating people about the safety of vaccines. A recent survey study by the CDC found that 90 percent of pregnant women had made a decision about whether they would vaccinate their child by the time they were six months along. While some may prefer posting a comment or sharing an article online, sometimes in-person dialogue is more effective, particularly when it comes to a personal topic such as child vaccination. Nelson noted, "I do think they appreciate it when you meet them sympathetically and you don't just try and blast facts down their throat."[2]

1. Quoted in Alex Olgin, "A Parent-to-Parent Campaign to Get Vaccine Rates Up," NPR, February 20, 2019. www.npr.org/sections/health-shots/2019/02/20/696259456/a-parent-to-parent-campaign-to-get-vaccine-rates-up.

2. Quoted in Olgin, "A Parent-to-Parent Campaign."

Parents are more likely to accept the established facts surrounding vaccination when someone they like and trust, such as a good friend, talks to them in person and does not dismiss their concerns for their child's safety.

the 1980s. It was not until the late 1990s, though, that these worries began to attract widespread media attention. In 1998, a British researcher named Andrew Wakefield led a study that was published in the British medical journal the *Lancet* alleging that a chemical called thimerosal that was present in the MMR vaccine might be contributing to rising rates of autism in children. Thimerosol is a preservative that contains trace (extremely tiny) amounts of mercury, a naturally occurring element that can be toxic to humans and other animals at high levels of exposure. At the time, thimerosol was used as a preservative in a number of important vaccines, including those for diphtheria, tetanus, pertussis, Hib, and hepatitis B.

One year later, the U.S. Public Health Service (PHS), the AAP, and vaccine manufacturers announced their intention to phase out the use of thimerosal in all childhood vaccines as soon as possible. This was accomplished by 2001; however, some seasonal flu vaccines still contain thimerosal because it prevents bacteria and fungi from growing in the vaccine. The organizations emphasized that they had found no evidence that the presence of thimerosal had caused any health problems for vaccinated children. They assured Americans that the vaccines were very safe because the human body can eliminate thimerosal quickly and easily, and that removing it from vaccines was just a way to make parents feel less concerned about them. Some parents and pediatricians who had heard about Wakefield's accusations, though, were alarmed. In their minds, wrote Kirby, "the government and the AAP were posing an extraordinary contradiction. If thimerosol exposure had been so minimal, and if there was no evidence of harm, then why call for its removal 'as soon as possible'?"[40]

Andrew Wakefield's research came under intense criticism following its release in 1998. In 2004, it was revealed that Wakefield's paper featured patients who had been recruited by a lawyer who was already involved in a lawsuit against vaccine manufacturers. Wakefield was also accused of falsifying his data to provide a link between autism and vaccines. Ten of Wakefield's twelve coauthors eventually withdrew their support for the paper. In 2010, Britain's General Medical Council ruled that Wakefield had engaged in misconduct during the course of conducting and publishing the study. Wakefield was banned from practicing medicine in Britain, and the *Lancet* formally retracted (withdrew support for) its 1998 publication of his paper.

There are two kinds of mercury compounds. Shown here is methylmercury, a metallic liquid that is very dangerous and stays in the human body for a long time. The type of mercury that is used to make thimerosal is called ethylmercury. Small amounts are not dangerous, and the body can eliminate it quickly. Most people who are concerned about vaccines causing mercury poisoning are not aware of the differences between methylmercury and ethylmercury.

However, since that time, other scientists have published their own faulty research alleging that vaccines are unsafe. While the theory that they cause autism has been thoroughly disproven, some people who claim to be experts have self-published their own books or created their own websites to spread misinformation. Some people believe these individuals' opinions carry more weight because they are not receiving money from Big Pharma. However, other organizations have their own reasons to provide financial support to people who are willing to back up their opinions, so going against the pharmaceutical industry is not an indication that someone has nothing to gain by publishing their opinions. Presenting these opinions as scientific research makes them seem more legitimate, which can be confusing for people who do not have much practice interpreting research articles and checking them for accuracy.

The Anti-Vax Movement Gains Steam

By the early 2000s, an organized anti-vax movement had taken shape. Groups led by concerned parents in Europe, Canada, Australia, the United States, and other parts of the world demanded further testing of childhood vaccines to see whether they were responsible for rising rates of autism, ADHD, and other childhood health disorders. Many of these same protesters also claimed that government vaccination requirements violated people's personal freedoms. Some of the most prominent of these anti-vaccine groups in the United States included Talk About Curing Autism (TACA), Generation Rescue, and the National Vaccine Information Center (NVIC).

The anti-vax movement has spread its message through books, television shows, and other traditional media. Much of its growth and influence, however, has been due to its effective use of the internet. Numerous anti-vax websites emerged during the 2000s, and their warnings struck a chord with a lot of parents. "In this new world," observed the PBS news program *Frontline*, "many parents are no longer willing to take the word of their doctor on faith, or to accept the conclusions of the medical establishment."[41]

A Closer Look

WHO listed the anti-vax movement as one of the top 10 global health threats of 2019, along with air pollution, antibiotic resistance, and diabetes.

To anti-vaxxers, these websites are a valuable resource. They say that the information contained on these websites exposes the lies and immoral behavior of the U.S. government and the health care industry on the issue of vaccination. They believe politicians and doctors only approve vaccines because they receive money from the pharmaceutical industry, which they say wants to sell vaccines regardless of any negative health effects on the people who receive them. They also claim that their websites give people the information they need to make an informed choice about vaccinating their children.

Physicians, disease experts, and public health officials, though, believe that these websites do more harm than good. "I think the internet has been

Fear and mistrust of the pharmaceutical industry has played a role in helping the anti-vax movement gain traction, especially after evidence surfaced showing that some drug companies were partially responsible for the current opioid crisis.

the fuel on the fire of anti-vaccine fears," said Arthur Caplan, the founder of the Division of Medical Ethics at New York University Langone Medical Center. "There's plenty of websites out there putting out information about people alleging all kinds of complications and problems with vaccines, their own pet theories about what might be dangerous about vaccines, so there are oodles of sources of lousy, dangerous information out there."[42]

People who oppose current vaccination practices have also made extensive use of public hearings to spread their message. These appearances in front of lawmakers often feature dramatic and emotional testimony from parents who genuinely believe that vaccines are the source of their child's health or development problems.

Censorship in the Battle Against Misinformation

In March 2019, the AMA issued a letter to the CEOs of leading social media companies, including Facebook, Twitter, YouTube, Pinterest, and others, urging them to combat the spread of anti-vaccine propaganda and ensure that the users of their platforms have access to accurate information.

"As physicians, we are concerned that the proliferation [spread] of this type of health-related misinformation will undermine sound science, further decrease vaccinations, and persuade people to make medical decisions that could spark the spread of easily preventable diseases," wrote Dr. James L. Madara, executive vice president and CEO of the AMA. "With public health on the line and with social media serving as a leading source of information for the American people, we urge you to do your part to ensure that users have access to scientifically valid information on vaccinations, so they can make informed decisions about their families' health."[1]

In response to the letter, many of the social media companies began banning certain content, advertisements, search terms, and hashtags, which some anti-vaxxers claim violates their First Amendment rights and limits alternative views. Whether companies have a responsibility to monitor the content shared on their platforms as well as whether they have the right to censor users who promote false information are sure to be ongoing issues in the coming years, particularly as epidemics of dangerous and preventable illnesses continue to crop up across the country.

1. James L. Madara to CEOs of Leading Technology Companies, March 13, 2019, American Medical Association. www.ama-assn.org/system/files/2019-03/madara-vaccination-letter.pdf.

In 2005, for example, activist Elizabeth Birt appeared before a special health committee of the Illinois General Assembly to tell lawmakers about her son. According to Birt, her son was a happy and healthy little boy until he received two vaccinations—an MMR vaccine and a Hib vaccine that contained thimerosol. From that point forward, her son's health declined rapidly and he stopped interacting with the world around him. "We waited and watched and hoped," she recalled. "My son's condition only worsened.

Actress Jenny McCarthy has been vocal about her belief that vaccines caused her son to develop autism, despite the fact that there is no scientific proof to back up her claims. Her visibility has contributed to the growing popularity of the anti-vax movement.

He started screaming uncontrollably and rubbing his stomach. It was like watching a fire die out ember by ember and there was no professional who could tell me how my child who had been so full of life and interactive was now in a world of his own."[43] These kinds of emotional narratives can be incredibly persuasive, regardless of their rationality or scientific support—a phenomenon social scientists refer to as "identifiable victim effect." Despite such accounts, some members of the movement insist that they are not necessarily interested in eliminating vaccines. "Please understand that we are not an antivaccine group," said Generation Rescue president Jenny McCarthy. "We are demanding safe vaccines. We want to reduce the schedule and reduce the toxins."[44]

Protecting Public Health

Despite numerous scientific studies demonstrating the safety and effectiveness of vaccines, concerns continue to rise and spread across social media websites and within communities. Russian internet trolls have added fuel to the vaccination debate by sharing the most extreme opinions on both sides on Twitter, according to a 2019 study by George Washington University; experts say these trolls aim to increase tension and divisiveness between separate groups within the United States, as they did in 2016 by sharing extreme points of view about the presidential election on social media. Meanwhile, Facebook has announced that it will take action against posts that spread verifiable misinformation about vaccines. As state governments struggle to contain disease outbreaks across the country, doctors and health officials wonder what else they can do to encourage parents to vaccinate their children.

"At the end of the day, it's values—beliefs about what matters, what's important, what should guide our lives and societies—that are most important," explained Gregory E. Kaebnick and Michael Gusmano in an article for *Slate*. They continued,

> *Values are not ignored in the vaccine debate; claims about parents' rights and harms to children are common. But too often, the pro-vaccination discourse [conversation] fails to recognize or thoroughly explore the role they play in the discussion, and in parents' minds. Whether it's doctors talking to patients, experts writing for the public, public health messages designed to increase the vaccination rate,*

or ordinary citizens posting on Facebook, just arguing about the facts won't get at what's really driving debate.[45]

The key, then, is to not simply repeat scientific facts that counter anti-vax arguments. There are several factors at play here. One is called information avoidance or confirmation bias, which is people's tendency to either ignore certain evidence that disproves their beliefs or seek out only information that confirms them. Carnegie Mellon University explained:

Questionable evidence is often treated as credible when it confirms what someone wants to believe—as is the case of discredited research linking vaccines to autism. And evidence that meets the rigorous demands of science is often discounted if it goes against what people want to believe, as illustrated by widespread dismissal of scientific evidence of climate change.[46]

Another factor involves people rejecting the evidence they are shown and clinging more firmly to their originally held beliefs because they do not want to feel that they were wrong. The popular truTV series *Adam Ruins Everything* discussed this in August 2017. The show, which is intended to show people that things they believe may actually be wrong, aired a segment about what it called "the backfire effect":

One study found that when people concerned about side effects of the flu shot were informed it was safe, they actually became less willing to get it … Because when you try to change someone's mind, the other person often feels attacked … Being proven wrong hurts so much, it often causes a fight or flight response.[47]

This is why people who hold a particular belief that is reinforced by the news they read or watch will often discount contradictory information and see it as evidence of bias, even when it is not. A large part of this is an unwillingness to feel unintelligent or easily tricked. For parents who are unwilling to get their children vaccinated, it generally also has to do with a combination of a desire to keep their children safe and a fear of the unknown. They believe they know what will happen if their child gets a particular disease, but they do not know if their child will have a negative reaction to a vaccine, so in their minds, getting the disease begins to seem like the better option— one that gives them more control over their child's health and safety.

Parents want to keep their children safe and healthy whenever possible, but they know they cannot always control this. For some, the anti-vax movement gives them the illusion of increased control, allowing them to feel less nervous about their children's health.

Although efforts to stop the spread of misinformation can help prevent further confusion, arguments that focus on mythbusting and appeals for "science-based" policies are more likely to put anti-vaxxers on the defensive rather than persuade them to change their minds. Christopher Graves, founder and president of the Ogilvy Center for Behavioral Science, said, "Instead, we need to dispel rumors and debunk myths without repeating the misinformation; rely on a compelling, proactive narrative; and realize that more information is not necessarily better."[48]

NOTES

Introduction: The Best Defense Is a Good Offense

1. "A History of Vaccines," PATH, April 2015. path.azureedge.net/media/documents/VAC_history_fs_2015.pdf.

Chapter One: How Vaccination Changed History

2. Arthur Allen, *Vaccine: The Controversial Story of Medicine's Greatest Lifesaver*. New York, NY: W. W. Norton, 2007, p. 28.

3. Quoted in Karie Youngdahl, "American Presidents and Infectious Diseases," History of Vaccines, July 3, 2013. www.historyofvaccines.org/content/blog/american-presidents-and-infectious-diseases.

4. Quoted in Allen, *Vaccine*, pp. 44–45.

5. Quoted in "Waterhouse Brings Vaccination to the States," History of Vaccines, accessed on May 14, 2019. www.historyofvaccines.org/content/waterhouse-brings-vaccination-states.

6. Quoted in William Howitt, *The History of the Supernatural in All Ages and Nations and in All Churches Christian and Pagan*. Philadelphia, PA: J.B. Lippincott, 1863, p. 241.

7. Genevieve Miller, ed., *Letters of Edward Jenner*. Baltimore, MD: Johns Hopkins University Press, 1983, p. 38.

8. Allen, *Vaccine*, p. 60.

9. Quoted in Allen, *Vaccine*, p. 73.

10. Kevin Hillstrom, *U.S. Health Politics and Policy: A Documentary History*. Washington, DC: CQ Press, 2011, p. 214.

11. Quoted in Allen, *Vaccine*, p. 136.

12. Allen, *Vaccine*, p. 118.

13. James Colgrove, *State of Immunity: The Politics of Vaccination in Twentieth-Century America*. Berkeley, CA: University of California Press, 2006, p. 117.

14. Quoted in Victoria Sherrow, *Makers of Modern Science: Jonas Salk*. New York, NY: Facts On File, 1993, p. 110.

15. Ananya Mandal, "Vaccine History," News-Medical.net, last updated February 27, 2019. www.news-medical.net/health/Vaccine-History.aspx.

16. "Making the Vaccine Decision," CDC, last updated March 18, 2019. www.cdc.gov/vaccines/parents/vaccine-decision/index.html.

17. Quoted in Melissa Curtin, "DTaP Vaccine Causes Brain Damage in Ten Month Old After 12 Hours," Stop Mandatory Vaccination, March 2, 2019. www.stopmandatoryvaccination.com/parent/vaccine-injury/dtap-vaccine-causes-brain-damage-in-ten-month-old-after-12-hours/.

Chapter Two: An Introduction to Vaccines

18. "How Do Vaccines Work?," Healthy Children, last updated February 26, 2019. www.healthychildren.org/English/safety-prevention/immunizations/pages/How-do-Vaccines-Work.aspx.

19. "Why Are Childhood Vaccines So Important?," CDC, last updated May 16, 2018. www.cdc.gov/vaccines/vac-gen/howvpd.htm.

20. "Vaccine Types," National Institute of Allergy and Infectious Diseases, last updated April 3, 2012. www.niaid.nih.gov/research/vaccine-types.

21. "Vaccine Types," National Institute of Allergy and Infectious Diseases.

22. "Different Types of Vaccines," History of Vaccines, last updated January 17, 2018. www.historyofvaccines.org/content/articles/different-types-vaccines.

23. Quoted in Susan Brink, "The Unintended Benefits of Vaccines," NPR, March 4, 2019. www.npr.org/sections/goatsandsoda/2019/03/04/699328555/the-unintended-benefits-of-vaccines.

24. "Vaccine Types," National Institute of Allergy and Infectious Diseases.

25. Quoted in "Microneedle Patch for Flu Vaccine," National Institutes of Health, July 25, 2017. www.nih.gov/news-events/nih-research-matters/microneedle-patch-flu-vaccine.

Chapter Three: Global Trends in Infectious Diseases

26. Quoted in Soumya Karlamangla, "Harvard-Westlake Students Were Vaccinated. Dozens Caught Whooping Cough Anyway," *Los Angeles Times*, March 16, 2019. www.latimes.com/local/california/la-me-ln-whooping-cough-vaccine-20190316-story.html.

27. Edith Bracho-Sanchez, "Chickenpox Parties and Natural Immunity: Your Questions Answered," CNN, March 22, 2019. www.cnn.com/2019/03/22/health/chickenpox-parties-need-to-know/index.html.

28. Jason Beaubien, "Chickenpox, the Latest Burden on the Rohingya Refugees," NPR, April 11, 2019. www.npr.org/sections/goatsandsoda/2019/04/11/711743116/chickenpox-the-latest-burden-for-the-rohingya-refugees.

29. "The End of the Line for Some Infectious Diseases?" in *Removing Obstacles to Healthy Development: World Health Organization Report on Infectious Diseases*. World Health Organization, 1999. www.who.int/infectious-disease-report/pages/ch6text.html.

30. Centers for Disease Control and Prevention, *Parent's Guide to Childhood Immunizations*. Atlanta, GA: CDC, 2016, p. 6. www.cdc.gov/vaccines/parents/tools/parents-guide/downloads/parents-guide-508.pdf.

31. "SAGE Issues Its 2018 Assessment Report of the Global Vaccine Action Plan," World Health Organization, last updated November 5, 2018. www.who.int/immunization/global_vaccine_action_plan/en/.

Chapter Four: Available Vaccines

32. "Misconceptions About Seasonal Flu and Flu Vaccines," CDC, last updated September 25, 2018. www.cdc.gov/flu/about/qa/misconceptions.htm.

33. Quoted in Marie Rosenthal, "Dispel Myths Among Members Who Fail to Get Their Flu Shots," *Managed Healthcare Executive*, November 1, 2011. www.managedhealthcareexecutive.com/member-engagement/dispel-myths-among-members-who-fail-get-their-flu-shots.

34. Quoted in Priyanka Boghani, "Dr. Paul Offit: 'A Choice Not To Get a Vaccine Is Not a Risk-Free Choice,'" PBS *Frontline*, March 23, 2015.

www.pbs.org/wgbh/frontline/article/paul-offit-a-choice-not-to-get-a-vaccine-is-not-a-risk-free-choice/.

35. Quoted in "Study Finds HPV Vaccine Has Lowered Number of Women with Disease," NPR, February 23, 2016. www.npr.org/2016/02/23/467840973/study-finds-hpv-vaccine-has-lowered-number-of-women-with-disease.

36. Quoted in "Study Finds HPV Vaccine," NPR.

Chapter Five: Going Viral

37. Quoted in Elizabeth Cohen, "Anti-Vaxers' Adult Son Gets Measles; Now, He Has This Message for the World," CNN, March 8, 2019. www.cnn.com/2019/03/07/health/measles-josh-nerius/index.html.

38. Quoted in Cohen, "Anti-Vaxers' Adult Son Gets Measles."

39. David Kirby, *Evidence of Harm: Mercury in Vaccines and the Autism Epidemic, a Medical Controversy*. New York, NY: St. Martin's Press, 2005, p. xiii.

40. Kirby, *Evidence of Harm*, p. 47.

41. Quoted in "The Vaccine War," PBS *Frontline*, 2010. www.pbs.org/wgbh/pages/frontline/vaccines/.

42. Quoted in "The Vaccine War," PBS *Frontline*.

43. Elizabeth Birt, testimony before Illinois General Assembly, November 17, 2005. www.adventuresinautism.blogspot.com/2005/12/liz-birt-1956-2005.html.

44. Quoted in Jeffrey Kluger, "Jenny McCarthy on Autism and Vaccines," *TIME*, April 1, 2009. www.time.com/time/health/article/0,8599,1888718,00.html#ixzz1ixwavtyQ.

45. Gregory E. Kaebnick and Michael Gusmano, "Forget About 'Because Science,'" *Slate*, April 15, 2019. slate.com/technology/2019/04/vaccination-values-science-based-policy.html.

46. Shilo Rea, "Information Avoidance: How People Select Their Own Reality," Carnegie Mellon University, March 13, 2017. www.cmu.edu/news/stories/archives/2017/march/information-avoidance.html.

47. truTV, "Adam Ruins Everything—Why Proving Someone Wrong Often Backfires," YouTube video, 1:39, August 24, 2017. www.youtube.com/watch?v=Q8NydsXl32s.

48. Christopher Graves, "Why Debunking Myths About Vaccines Hasn't Convinced Dubious Parents," *Harvard Business Review*, February 20, 2015. hbr.org/2015/02/why-debunking-myths-about-vaccines-hasnt-convinced-dubious-parents.

American Academy of Pediatrics (AAP)
345 Park Boulevard
Itasca, IL 60143
www.aap.org
twitter.com/AmerAcadPeds
> The AAP is North America's largest organization of pediatricians and other health care professionals who provide services to infants, children, and young adults.

American Public Health Association (APHA)
800 I Street NW
Washington, D.C. 20001
www.apha.org
twitter.com/PublicHealth
> APHA provides information on matters that affect public health, such as climate change, gun violence, and vaccinations.

Centers for Disease Control and Prevention (CDC)
1600 Clifton Road
Atlanta, GA 30333
www.cdc.gov
www.instagram.com/CDCgov
twitter.com/CDCgov
www.youtube.com/user/CDCstreamingHealth
> The CDC and its scientific researchers provide the federal government's first line of defense against outbreaks of infectious disease. The CDC maintains extensive information dedicated to vaccines and immunization programs.

Immunization Action Coalition (IAC)
2550 University Avenue West, Suite 415 North
Saint Paul, MN 55114
www.immunize.org
twitter.com/ImmunizeAction
www.youtube.com/user/ImmunizationAction

> The Immunization Action Coalition maintains a variety of websites, publications, handouts, and other materials designed to educate health care professionals and parents about the importance of immunization as well as the safety and effectiveness of individual vaccines.

FOR MORE INFORMATION

Books

Kinch, Michael. *Between Hope and Fear: A History of Vaccines and Human Immunity*. New York, NY: Pegasus Books, 2018.
> This book examines the science of immunity, the public policy implications of vaccine denial, and the real-world outcomes of failing to vaccinate.

Largent, Mark A. *Vaccine: The Debate in Modern America*. Baltimore, MD: Johns Hopkins University Press, 2012.
> This book takes a critical look at the vaccine debate, disentangling competing claims over their safety and providing recommendations for moving forward.

Mnookin, Seth. *The Panic Virus: The True Story Behind the Vaccine-Autism Controversy*. New York, NY: Simon & Schuster, 2012.
> In this detailed but accessible work of investigative journalism, the author draws on interviews with parents, public health advocates, scientists, and anti-vaccine activists to explore how fear can overwhelm logic—sometimes with devastating effects.

Ringstad, Arnold. *Medical Myths, Busted!*. North Mankato, MN: 12-Story Library, 2017.
> This book exposes the truth about 12 medical myths, including how they got started and who proved each one wrong.

Rissman, Rebecca. *The Vaccination Debate*. Minneapolis, MN: Essential Library, 2016.
> This book examines the controversy over vaccination and whether it qualifies as an issue of public safety or personal freedom.

Websites

Children's Hospital of Philadelphia (CHOP): Vaccine Education Center

www.chop.edu/service/vaccine-education-center/

> This section of the Children's Hospital of Philadelphia's website provides extensive information on all aspects of vaccination.

Healthy Children

healthychildren.org

> This website, which is maintained by the AAP, contains information on various health and safety issues pertaining to children and teens, including vaccination.

PATH: Vaccine Resource Library

www.path.org/vaccineresources

> This website is maintained by PATH, an international nonprofit organization that seeks to improve the health of communities around the world. The website contains information on immunization and infectious diseases.

Voices for Vaccines

www.voicesforvaccines.org

> This parent-led organization supports and advocates for on-time vaccination and the reduction of vaccine-preventable disease. Its aim is to provide families with evidence-based information about the safety and importance of immunization in a welcoming and supportive community environment.

INDEX

Food and Drug Administration
(FDA), 33, 44, 46, 73
formaldehyde, 38

G
Gardasil, 73
glycerin, 18
Graves, Christopher, 90
Guillain-Barré syndrome (GBS), 26
Gusmano, Michael, 87

H
Haemophilus influenzae type b
(Hib), 41–42, 50, 53, 71, 81, 85
Haffkine, Waldemar Mordecai, 19
hepatitis A, 40, 51, 53, 71
hepatitis B, 26, 40, 44, 50, 53, 71,
81
HepA vaccine, 71
HepB vaccine, 71
herd immunity, 37
Hillstrom, Kevin, 22
human papillomavirus (HPV), 40,
72–75
Hviid, Anders, 32

I
immune systems, 6, 9, 11–12,
35–40, 42, 44, 48, 62, 73
influenza, 21, 38, 44, 62, 64–66,
71
inoculation, 11, 13–15, 17
*Inquiry into the Causes and Effects of
the Variolae Vaccinae, An*
(Jenner), 17
insecticides, 24

J
Jackson, Andrew, 12
Jacobson v. Massachusetts (1905), 21
Jefferson, Thomas, 15, 17
Jenner, Edward, 15–17, 19

K
Kabir, Mohammad Ahsanul, 49
Kaebnick, Gregory E., 87
Kirby, David, 78, 81
Klein, Nicola P., 48
Koch, Robert, 18

L
laws, 7, 17–20, 23–24, 37, 48, 78
Lincoln, Abraham, 12

M
Madara, James L., 85
malaria, 24, 46, 60
Mather, Cotton, 11–13
McCarthy, Jenny, 32, 86–87
measles, 26, 31–32, 37, 40, 42,
54–56, 69, 77
meningitis, 41, 53, 55, 57
mercury, 14, 81–82
Mickelson, Amanda, 33
microneedle patches, 44–45
Mina, Michael, 42
MMR vaccine, 32, 38, 69, 71, 81,
85
MMRV vaccine, 71
mosquitoes, 24, 46, 70
mumps, 31–32, 40, 55, 69

N
nasal sprays, 44, 73
National Childhood Vaccine Injury
Act, 33
National Institute of Allergy and
Infectious Diseases (NIAID), 36,
38
Nelson, Kim, 80
Nerius, Joshua, 77
Nichols, Janice Flood, 28

O
Offit, Paul, 67

PICTURE CREDITS

ABOUT THE AUTHOR

Michelle Harris has worked for several years as a digital content writer, creating informational and marketing materials for television, online news, and consumer products. She received a bachelor of arts degree in psychology from the University of California at Santa Barbara. Her other published works include *HPV: Prevention and Treatment* and *Schizophrenia: When Reality Becomes Distorted*.